PROBLEMS OF ETHICS

BY

MORITZ SCHLICK

TRANSLATED AND WITH A NEW INTRODUCTION

By

DAVID RYNIN, Ph.D.

Department of Philosophy
University of California

DOVER PUBLICATIONS, INC.
NEW YORK

Manufactured in the United States of America

Dover Publications, Inc.
180 Varick Street
New York 14, N. Y.

INTRODUCTION TO DOVER EDITION

THE appearance in the Dover reprint series of this
book on ethics by Moritz Schlick (1882-1936) — the
leader in its most influential period of the scientifically
oriented philosophical movement that came to be known
as logical positivism — has a special appropriateness,
by virtue of the predominantly scientific character of
the distinguished works that constitute the series and
because of the general outlook of the author on ethical
questions, which was, in the best sense of the word,
scientific.[1] This is not to say that he was under the
mistaken impression that progress in natural science
would solve the problems of morals, but rather that he
approached these problems with the scientific aim of
giving an *explanation* of moral conduct, of why men
act morally.

In this he distinguished himself from many of his
contemporaries and much of the established tradition
by considering the role of the moralist, the prophet,
the creator of a new morality, as one to be sharply

---

[1] In fact, the original edition of this book (Vienna 1930, J. Springer
Verlag) appeared under the title *Fragen der Ethik* as Volume 4 of a
series entitled *Schriften zur wissenschaftlichen Weltauffassung;* that is,
as a book conceived as a contribution to a scientific world-view.

separated from that of the philosopher. With respect
to the latter he rejected the view characteristic of most
(of at least Anglo-American) moral philosophy of the
twentieth century; namely, that the philosopher's business with ethics is simply and exclusively that of giving
an adequate analysis or explanation of the meaning of
its fundamental terms or concepts. To confuse a study
of morality with exhortation to moral conduct was in
his view to make very improbable the solution of the
problems of either the moralist or the philosopher; and
to suppose that the basic task of the latter was to
establish a concept delimiting the domain of moral
phenomena he deemed to be mistaken, and the task
a work of supererogation, since in his opinion these
phenomena are for the most part as familiar to men
as are, to use his example, the phenomena of light that
constitute the subject matter of optics. He did not
reject wholly the relevance, to an understanding of
ethical conduct, of an examination of ethical concepts,
but he considered this at best a preliminary task to that
of gaining *knowledge about* ethical phenomena, a task
presupposing that the subject matter of ethics is already
on the whole well known and its concepts understood.

Schlick, in fact, considers his work in ethics a mixture
of philosophical analysis (meaning clarification) and,
in the broad sense, psychology; he directs some rather
sharp remarks against those philosophers who might
deem a concern with psychological questions unphil-
osophical. Is this attitude of disdain or contempt not

perhaps one based on their desire to be freed of many burdensome facts of psychology as they go about constructing their philosophical ethical systems? "If we decide that the fundamental question of ethics, 'Why does man act morally?' can be answered only by psychology, we see in this no degradation of, nor injury to, science, but a happy simplification of the world-picture. In ethics we do not seek independence, but only the truth." (p. 30)

But Schlick is not one of those who suppose that ethics rests on psychology by virtue of our learning what is morally good from an observation of human desire. It is not psychology that tells us what the moral good is; rather the content of the concept is determined by society. And psychology's role is simply this: it gives us the knowledge that *explains* how individual human desire is brought into conformity with what society demands of us, i.e., what it deems good. If one condemns the judgment of society as to what is morally good, as men of outstanding moral insight and vision must sometimes do, this condemnation is that of the creative moralist, not that of the moral philosopher. The moral philosopher's task is to make intelligible the often astonishing facts of moral behaviour, not to reformulate or raise to a higher level the moral insights and standards of a people — although the latter task is an achievement that is obviously of inestimable worth. It is no condemnation of Jesus or Buddha that they were not moral philosophers, but wise men and saints.

Of course nothing prevents a man from being at times a prophet as well as a philosopher.

In this small work the author throws much light on many traditional questions of ethics. His criticism of the doctrine of absolute values and intuitionism, his emendation of utilitarianism by way of overcoming the well-known difficulties involved in a felicific calculus, his shrewd psychological analysis of the prejudice against pleasure, as well as numerous highly illuminating considerations dealing with the problems of motivation, freedom and responsibility, egoism, and the sources of human value mark him as an original and profound thinker in this field — a field to which he alone among the positivists gave much thought and in which he showed what could be done by approaching the study of ethics in the scientific spirit.

The availability once again of this work has also a certain timeliness in view of the prevailing notion that the underlying standpoint of modern positivism rendered it incompetent to deal with ethical questions or, what perhaps comes to the same thing, forced it into the absurd position of maintaining that ethical questions were devoid of cognitive meaning, that ethical discourse was some sort of nonsense, or at best purely expressive or evocative in function, akin to animal outcries of approval or disapproval, or on a higher level, more or less akin to poetic expressions of ideals and longings, or power drives, hence in no sense either true or false. For Schlick is distinguished by his unqualified and unambiguous rejection of precisely that view of ethics more or less correctly attributed to others of the school, such as H. Reichenbach and R. Carnap, and shared by such an eminent scientific philosopher as Bertrand Russell, who in his later writings holds that there can be no science (knowledge, in the proper sense) of values, including ethical values.

The typical criticism leveled against the movement in which Schlick played so prominent a role, and whose fundamental position was derived from a conception of meaning and meaningfulness closely connected with the needs and interests of natural science — I refer to the so-called verifiability principle — was that it could not make sense of, let alone do justice to, normative issues. It was held, in short, that one who maintains the view that cognitively meaningful discourse consists solely of utterances that are empirically verifiable or falsifiable, or perhaps confirmable or disconfirmable by experience, would have to abandon as meaningless, statements about good and evil, right and wrong, and the like, not to speak of those dealing with metaphysical problems, alleged or thought to deal with matters lying beyond all possible experience, hence beyond empirical testing.

Such a critical view of the implications of the central tenet of this movement for matters of perennial philosophic concern could, however, be made (and was made) plausible in general only by ignoring the writings of Schlick, who took an opposite line, not merely with

respect to the nature of ethical discourse but of metaphysical discourse as well, except in a special — and
according to him not the ordinary — sense of that much
abused term "metaphysics." Contrary to the widely
held view, the principles of logical positivism do not
require that ethics (or even metaphysics) be void of
cognitive content. And the appearance of the present
work may serve in part to correct the widespread mis-
apprehension on this point.

It may also in some degree serve as a kind of corrective to the excessively one-sided conception of the nature
of ethical discourse expounded and defended by many
able members of the influential school of "ordinary
language philosophers" who have in recent years flour-
ished in England and especially Oxford, and whose
views have been powerfully exploited elsewhere in the
English-speaking world. These thinkers, if not deriving
from the logical positivists, at least have in Ludwig
Wittgenstein a common source of inspiration with them.
Wittgenstein's *Tractatus Logico-Philosophicus* was a
kind of bible to the Viennese School, and his later work
was the source of many of the insights of the Oxford
group. He exercised a very strong influence on Schlick
during the period preceding the writing of *Fragen der
Ethik,* if not on the subject matter of this book at least
in relation to the conception of philosophy as an activity
of making meanings clear, and on Schlick's views on
many topics falling in the province of theory of knowledge, the subject in which his main reputation had been

made earlier. (His important *Allgemeine Erkenntnis-lehre,* a work unfortunately never translated, is probably the best general work in the theory of knowledge to appear in this century, and is still very much worth careful study.)

Reacting to the exclusive concern of the positivists with the cognitive, descriptive (scientific) function of language, these later thinkers have stressed its practical, nontheoretical functions, and in their opposition to the earlier views have frequently so overstated their insights as to render them rather less valid and useful than they might otherwise have been. They have, by and large, gone to the extreme of denying any cognitive content whatever to ethical discourse, adopting the view that it serves primarily if not exclusively other functions, such as advising or commending, thus putting almost exclusive emphasis on what may be called, in a wide sense of the term, its *rhetorical* aspect — ignoring, unfortunately, what the best students of rhetoric understood very well — namely, the fact that nothing is as persuasive in the long run as the truth. While sharing with Schlick a general conception of philosophizing as meaning clarification (analysis), these thinkers differ from him in supposing that philosophical concern with ethical discourse is centered wholly upon making meanings clear, interpreting a study of the meaning of ethical concepts as the study of the non-descriptive *use* of ethical terms. The reader may find in *Problems of Ethics* a useful contrast to these often oversubtle and on the whole antirational views. In any event, a comparison of the two differing approaches to ethics cannot help but cast some light into a discipline not always distinguished for that quality.

David Rynin
Department of Philosophy
University of California

Berkeley, California
May, 1961

Foreword

THE appearance, in English translation, of Professor
Moritz Schlick's *Fragen der Ethik* is timely and
welcome. Professor Schlick was the leader of the
vigorous and influential "Vienna Circle," a group of
scientists, logicians, and philosophers who attacked in
a fresh way the persistent problem as to what the
nature and the significant function of philosophical
reflection really is. These thinkers, in general, carry
on the traditions of empiricism and positivism, which
they have reformulated in the light of certain views
arising from a logical analysis of language and symbols. Accordingly, the position which these writers
represent sometimes goes by the name of "logical
positivism." The application of the methods and results of this type of analysis to some of the traditional
problems of ethics supplies the substance of this book.
It will bring home to the mind of the thoughtful
reader the pressing question as to the real nature of
ethical problems—indeed of all those problems which
have to do with the appraisal of human values. These
problems are crucial for us now, both in theory and in
practice. To have so unambiguous and clear a state-

ment of these problems as they appear within the perspective of modern positivism is very much worth while.

GEORGE P. ADAMS

The University of California

Translator's Note

ALTHOUGH this authorized translation of Moritz Schlick's *Fragen der Ethik* was read and approved, and in part revised, by the author before his untimely and tragic death, I accept full responsibility for whatever shortcomings may yet characterize it. I wish to thank my friends for their assistance in rendering the more difficult passages into readable English.

DAVID RYNIN

Contents

Preface[1]

ETHICS is generally considered to be a part of philosophy. But according to the view here represented, philosophy is not a science, that is, it is not a system of propositions. Its task consists in making clear the content of scientific propositions, that is, in determining or discovering their meaning. The final determination of the meaning of propositions cannot itself be made by means of assertions, cannot thus itself form a science, because in that case we would have to ask ever anew for the meaning of the explanatory proposition, and would thus arrive at an infinite regress. Every statement of a meaning (called "definition") must, generally through a series of sub-definitions, finally lead to a direct exhibition of what is meant. This exhibition can only be the result of an actual operation, a physical or psychic *act*. Thus the determination of the ultimate meaning is always the result of an *activity*. This activity constitutes the essence of philosophy; there are no philosophical propositions, but only philosophical acts.

---

[1] [The irrelevant first paragraph of the original is omitted.]

How, then, is a philosophical book possible at all, since one cannot put activities into the pages of a book? What can a treatise on ethics contain? For if ethics really were philosophy it could consist only of those acts by means of which the meaning of moral judgments would be discovered and explained.

Concerning this, two things are to be said.

First, in so far as this treatise is "philosophical" (and it would like actually to make such a claim), its sentences function not as actual propositions which communicate definite facts or laws, but as stimuli for the reader to carry out those acts by virtue of which certain propositions obtain a clear meaning. (That such stimuli can be much more important than any correct judgments can be disputed by no one who believes in the power of philosophy.) Those propositions are such as occur in daily life (for example, "This man is well-intentioned"; "That man was completely responsible for his act."); they will not be formulated in this treatise, but constitute the subject-matter for consideration.

In the second place, however, the book would like to claim for certain of its sentences that they are real propositions. Thus I believe that in the following pages I communicate some truths—in my opinion not unimportant ones. If this is not an illusion, the book may also be called scientific, for, according to what was said previously, true judgments may be systematized; they constitute a part of science. Since those propositions concern the behavior of men, the scientific field to which they belong is *psychology*.

I hope, then, to have contributed, first, to philosophical activity and, secondly, to psychological knowledge by the answers which the book gives to fundamental ethical problems, and by the observations leading to these answers. This contribution points to a very different orientation from that which now prevails in the literature of German moral philosophy —and seems to me for this reason all the more important.

MORITZ SCHLICK

Vienna, September 1930.

CHAPTER I

What Is the Aim of Ethics?

1. *Ethics Seeks Nothing But Knowledge*

If there are ethical questions which have meaning, and are therefore capable of being answered, then ethics is a science. For the correct answers to its questions will constitute a system of true propositions, and a system of true propositions concerning an object is the "science" of that object. Thus ethics is a system of *knowledge,* and nothing else; its only goal is the truth. Every science is, as such, purely theoretical; it seeks to understand; hence the questions of ethics, too, are purely theoretical problems. As philosophers we try to find their correct solutions, but their practical application, if such is possible, does not fall within the sphere of ethics. If anyone studies these questions in order to apply the results to life and action, his *dealing* with ethics has, it is true, a practical end; but ethics itself never has any other goal than the truth.

So long as the philosopher is concerned with his purely theoretical questions, he must forget that he has a human interest as well as a cognitive interest in the object of his investigation. For him there is no greater

danger than to change from a philosopher into a moralist, from an investigator into a preacher. Desire for
the truth is the only appropriate inspiration for the
thinker when he philosophizes; otherwise his thoughts
run the danger of being led astray by his feelings.
His wishes, hopes, and fears threaten to encroach upon
that objectivity which is the necessary presupposition
of all honest inquiry. Of course, the prophet and the
investigator can be one and the same person; but one
cannot at the same moment serve both interests, for
whoever mixes the two problems will solve neither.

A glance at the great ethical systems will show how
necessary these remarks are. There is hardly one in
which we do not occasionally find an appeal to the
feeling or the morality of the reader where a scientific
analysis would have been appropriate.

Nevertheless, I do not point out the purely theoretical character of ethics merely to warn my reader, and
myself. I do it also because it will help us to define
the problems with which ethics is concerned and which
we shall try to solve.

2. The Subject-matter of Ethics

To what object, or realm of objects, do the questions
of ethics relate? This object has many names, and we
use them so often in daily life that one might think we
should know exactly what we mean by them. The
ethical questions concern "morality," or what is morally "valuable," what serves as a "standard" or "norm"

of human conduct, what is "demanded" of us; or, finally, to name it by the oldest, simplest word, ethical questions concern the "good."

And what does ethics do with this object? We have already answered this question: ethics seeks to *understand* it, to gain knowledge of it, and would and can under no circumstances do anything else with it. Since ethics is, in essence, theory or knowledge, its task cannot be to produce morality, or to establish it, or call it to life. It does not have the task of producing the good—neither in the sense that its business is to invest the good with reality in human affairs, nor in the sense that it has to stipulate or decree what the word "good" ought to signify. It creates neither the concept nor the objects which fall under the concept, nor does it provide the opportunity of applying the concept to the objects. All this it finds, as every science finds the materials it works with, in experience. It is obvious that no science can have any other beginning. The misleading view (introduced by the "Neo-Kantians") according to which objects of a science are not simply "given" to it but are themselves always "given as problems" will not lead anyone to deny that whoever wishes to understand anything must first know *what* it is he wishes to understand.

Where and how, then, is "the good" of ethics given?

We must from the outset be clear on the point that here there is only *one* possibility, the same that lies before all other sciences. Wherever an instance of the object to be known occurs, there must be exhibited a certain mark (or group of marks) which characterizes the thing or event as one of a certain definite kind, thus distinguishing it from all others in a special way. If this were not so we would have no opportunity and no motive to call it by a special name. Every name which is used in discourse for communication must have a meaning capable of being indicated. This is indeed self-evident, and it would not be doubted of the object of any other science—only in ethics has it sometimes been forgotten.

Let us consider some examples outside the field of ethics. Biology, the science of life, finds its sphere limited by a group of characteristics (a special kind of motion, regeneration, growth, and so forth) which belong to all living things, and stand out so clearly for every-day observation that—apart from certain critical instances—the difference between the animate and inanimate is very sharply distinguished, without the use of any scientific analysis. It is only because of this that the concept of life could have first been formed, and obtained its special name. If the biologist succeeds, with progressive knowledge, in establishing new and sharper definitions of life, in order better to bring the events of life under general laws, this means only more precision in, and perhaps extension of, the concept, without however altering its original meaning.

Similarly the word "light" had a definite meaning before there was a science of light, that is, optics, and this meaning determined the subject-matter of optics. The distinguishing mark was in this case that immediate experience which we call "light-sensation," that is, a not-further-definable datum of consciousness, known only to the perceiver, the occurrence of which—again apart from critical instances—indicates the presence of those events which constitute the subject-matter of optics. The fact that optics in its modern developed form is the science of Roentgen rays and radio-telegraphic waves as well (because their laws are identical with the laws of light) enlarges the meaning of the word "optics" without changing its basis.

As certainly, then, as the expression "moral good" makes good sense, just as certainly must we be able to discover it in a way analogous to that by which one discovers the meaning of the word "life" or "light." But many philosophers see in this a serious difficulty of ethics, indeed *the* difficulty, and they are of the opinion that the sole task of ethics is the discovery of the definition of "good."

3. *On the Definition of Good*

This view can be interpreted in two ways. In the first place, it could mean that the task of the philosopher is exhausted in describing exactly the sense in which the word "good"—or *bon* or *gut* or *buono* or ἀγαθόν—in its moral signification is actually used. It would concern itself merely with making clear the already well-known meaning, by a strict formulation of it in other words (were it not already well known one would not know that, for example, "good" is the translation of *bonum*). Is this really the goal of ethics? The statement of the meaning of words by definitions is (as G. E. Moore in his *Principia Ethica* has pointed out in a similar connection) the business of the science of language. Ought we really to believe that ethics is a branch of linguistics? Perhaps a branch that has split off from it because the definition of "good" harbors special difficulties we meet in no other word? A very peculiar case, that a whole science should be necessary to find merely the definition of a concept! And in any case, who is interested in mere definitions? They are, after all, only means to an end; they stand at the *beginning* of the real cognitive task. If ethics ended with a definition it would be at most the introduction to a science, and the philosopher would interest himself only in what comes after it. No, the real problems of ethics are certainly of a very different sort. Even though the task of ethics could be formulated as that of stating what the good "really is," this could not be understood as consisting in the mere determination of the meaning of a concept (as also, in our example, optics does not strive for a mere definition of "light"). Rather it would have to be understood as the task of explanation, of complete cognition of the good—which presupposes that the meaning of the concept is already known and then relates it to something else, orders it in more general connections (just as optics does with light, which tells us what light "really is" by pointing out the place in the sphere of natural events to which the well-known phenomenon belongs, by describing to the last detail its laws, and by recognizing their identity with the laws of certain electrical events).

Secondly, the view according to which the goal of ethics consists of a correct determination of the concept "good" could be interpreted as not being concerned with the formulation of the content of the concept, but rather with giving it a content. This would, however, be exactly that view which we have from the start recognized to be quite senseless. It would mean that the philosopher made, or created, the concept of the good, while without him there existed merely the word "good." He would of course have to invent it quite arbitrarily. (But inasmuch as in formulating his definition he could not act completely arbitrarily, since he would be bound by some norm, some guiding principle, the concept of the good would already be determined by these norms. The philosopher would have merely to find a formulation of it, and we should have before us the previously considered case.) However, it would be quite absurd to demand of ethics nothing but the arbitrary establishment of the meaning of a word. That would be no achievement at all. Even the prophet, the creator of a new morality, never forms a new concept of morality, but presupposes one, and asserts only that other modes of behavior are subsumed under it than those which people have believed up to that time. In logical terms, the prophet holds that the acknowledged content of the concept has a different range from that supposed. This alone can be the meaning when he declares: "Not that is 'good' which you have held as such, but something else!"

Thus we see the view confirmed that in no way is the formulation of the concept of the moral good to be considered as the final task of ethics; it cannot be regarded as anything but a mere preparation.

To be sure, this preparation is not to be neglected; ethics ought not to spare itself the task of determining the meaning of its concept, even though, as we have said, the meaning of the word "good" may in one sense be assumed as known.

4. *Is the Good Indefinable?*

It is very dangerous to withdraw from this task under the pretext that the word "good" is one of those whose meaning is simple and unanalyzable, of which therefore a definition, a statement of the connotation, is impossible. What is demanded here need not be a definition in the strictest sense of the word. It is sufficient to indicate how we can get the content of the concept; to state what must be done in order to become acquainted with its content. It is, strictly speaking, also impossible to define what the word "green" means —but we can nevertheless fix its meaning unambiguously, for example, by saying it is the color of a summer meadow, or by pointing to the foliage of a tree. We mentioned above that a "light-sensation" which furnishes us with the fundamental concept of optics is not definable; however, we know exactly what is meant by it, because we can give the exact conditions under which we have a light-sensation. In the same way, in ethics we must be able to give the exact conditions under which the word "good" is applied, even though — its fundamental concept be indefinable. In this manner it must be possible to give the meaning of any word, for otherwise it would have no meaning at all. It must even be capable of being given easily; profound philosophical analysis cannot be necessary for this, for the matter concerns merely a question of fact, namely, a description of those conditions under which the word "good" (or its equivalent in other languages, or its contrary, "evil") is actually used.

It is difficult for many philosophers to stick to the realm of facts even temporarily, without immediately inventing a theory to describe the facts. And thus the theory has been frequently propounded that the fundamental concept of ethics is given as is the fundamental concept of optics. Just as we possess a special sense, namely the sense of sight, for the perception of light, so it is supposed that a special "moral sense" indicates the presence of good or evil. Accordingly, good and evil would be objective characters, to be determined and investigated as are the physical events which optics investigates, and which it considers to be the causes of light-sensations.

This theory is of course wholly hypothetical. The — moral sense is merely assumed; its organs cannot be pointed out as can the human eye. But the hypothesis is also false; it fails to account for the variations in moral judgment among men, since the further assumption that the moral sense is poorly developed in many persons, or completely absent, does not suffice to explain these variations.

No, it is not the distinguishing characteristic of the subject-matter of ethics that it is the object of a special kind of perception. Its·characteristics must be capable of exhibition by simply pointing to certain known facts, without any artifice. This can happen in different ways. Two ways are here distinguished: first, one can seek for an external, formal characteristic of good and evil; and, second, one can search for a material characteristic, one of content.

5. *The Formal Characteristic of the Good*

The formal characteristic, on which Kant placed the whole weight of his moral philosophy, and which he made prominent by his greatest eloquence, is this: the good always appears as something that is demanded, or commanded; the evil, as something forbidden. Good conduct is such as is demanded or desired of us. Or, as it has generally been expressed since Kant: those actions are good which we *ought to do*. Now, to a demand, a claim, or a desire there belongs someone who demands, claims, or desires. This author of the moral law must also be given in order that the characterization by means of the formal property of the command be unambiguous.

Here opinions differ. In theological ethics this author is God, and according to one interpretation the good is good because God desires it; in this case the formal characteristic (to be a command of God) would express the very essence of the good. According to another, perhaps profounder, interpretation, God desires the good because it is good. In this case its essence must be given by certain material characters previously to and independently of those formal determinations. In traditional philosophical ethics the opinion prevails that the author is, for example, human society (utilitarianism) or the active self (eudaimonism) or even no one (the categorical imperative). From this last proceeds Kant's doctrine of the "absolute ought," that is, a demand without a demander. One of the worst errors of ethical thought lies in his belief that the concept of the moral good is completely exhausted by the statement of its purely formal property, that it has no content except to be what is demanded, "what should be."

6. *Material Characteristics*

In opposition to this, it is clear that the discovery of the formal characters of the good constitutes only a preliminary step in the determination of the content of the good, in the statement of material characteristics. If we know that the good is what is demanded, we must still ask: What is it then that is actually demanded? In answer to this question we must turn to the author of the command and investigate his will

and desire, for the content of his desire is that which
he wishes to happen. When I recommend an action to
someone as being "good," I express the fact that I
desire it.

So long as the lawgiver is not known with certainty,
we must stick to the laws as they are generally observed, to the formulations of moral rules as we find
them among men. We must discover which ways of
acting (or dispositions, or whatever be the term used)
are called "good" by different people, at different
times, by different wise men or religious writers. Only
in this way do we come to know the content of this
concept. From the content it may then be possible to
infer the lawgiving authority, if it cannot be ascer-
tained otherwise.

In grouping together the individual cases in which
something is designated as morally good, we must
search for the common elements, the characters in
which these examples agree or show similarities.
These similar elements are the characters of the concept "good"; they constitute its content, and within
them must lie the reason why one and the same word,
"good," is used for the several cases.

To be sure, one will at once come upon cases in
which nothing common can be found, in which there
seems to be a complete incompatibility; one and the
same thing—for example, polygamy—will be considered moral in one community, and in another a crime.
In such a situation there are two possibilities. First,
there could be several irreducibly different concepts of

"good" (which agree in the purely formal property of being somehow "demanded"); if this were so there would not be a single morality, but many. Or, second, it could be that the divergence in moral judgments was only apparent and not final; that, namely, in the end one and the same goal was approved, but that a difference of opinion prevailed as to which way leads to it, which actions should therefore be demanded. (For instance, polygamy and monogamy are not in themselves judged morally. The real object of valuation is perhaps the peace of family life, or the least troublesome order of sexual relationships. One person believes that this end can be attained only through monogamous marriage, and considers it, therefore, to be morally good; another believes the same of polygamy. One may be right, the other wrong; they differ, not by their final valuations, but only by virtue of their insight, capacity of judgment, or experience.)

Whether there is actually among men a multiplicity of moralities incompatible with one another, or whether the differences in the moral world are only specious, so that the philosopher would find everywhere, under the many disguises and masks of morality, one and the same face of the one Good, we cannot now decide. In any case, there are wide regions in which the unanimity and security of moral judgments is substantiated. The modes of behavior which we group together under the names reliability, helpfulness, sociability are everywhere judged to be "good," while, for example, thievery, murder, quarrelsomeness pass for "evil" so unanimously that here the question of the common property can be answered with practically universal validity. If such characters are found for a large group of actions, then one can apply himself to the "exceptions" and irregularities, that is, to those cases in which the same behavior evokes divergent moral judgments in different times, among different peoples. Here one finds either that there is no different ground for the judgment from that in all ordinary cases, but that it is merely more remote, hidden, or applied under altered circumstances; or one must simply note the fact as indicating a new or ambiguous meaning of the word "good." And finally, it happens, of course, that certain individuals hold different opinions regarding good and evil from those held by people of their time and community. In these cases it is quite as important to make out the content and causes of their opinions as in any other more regular cases, if the persons in question are important as prophets, moral writers, or morally creative men; or if their teachings disclose hidden currents or impress their moral judgments on humanity and the future.

7. Moral Norms and Moral Principles

The common characteristics which a group of "good" acts or dispositions exhibits can be combined in a *rule* of the form: A mode of action must have such and such properties in order to be called "good" (or "evil"). Such a rule can also be called a "norm." Let it be understood at once, however, that such a "norm" is nothing but a mere expression of fact; it gives us only the conditions under which an act or disposition or character is actually called "good," that is, is given a moral value. The setting up of norms is nothing but the determination of the concept of the good, which ethics undertakes to understand.

This determination would proceed by seeking ever new groups of acts that are recognized to be good, and showing for each of them the rule or norm which all of their members satisfy. The different norms, so obtained, would then be compared, and one would order them into new classes such that the individual norms of each class had something in common, and thus would all be subsumed under a higher, that is, a more general, norm. With this higher norm the same procedure would be repeated, and so on, until, in a perfect case, one would at last reach a highest, most general rule that included all others as special cases, and would be applicable to every instance of human conduct. This highest norm would be the definition of "the good" and would express its universal essence; it would be what the philosopher calls a "moral principle."

Of course, one cannot know beforehand whether one will actually arrive at a single moral principle. It might well be that the highest series of rules to which the described way leads simply shows no common character, that one has, therefore, to stop with several norms as highest rules, because despite all attempts none higher can be found to which these could be reduced. There would then be several mutually independent meanings of the expression "moral good," several mutually independent moral principles which only in their totality would determine the concept of morality, or perhaps several different concepts of the moral, depending upon the time and the people. It is significant how little these possibilities have, in general, been considered by philosophers; almost all have at once sought a single moral principle. Quite the contrary is true of the practical moral systems, which ordinarily do not attempt to establish an all-inclusive principle; as in the case of the catechism, which stops at the ten commandments.

For those who believe that the sole task of ethics consists in the determination of the concept of the good, that is, in the establishment of one or several moral principles, the completion of the described procedure would exhaust the theme of ethics. It would be a pure "normative science"; for its end would lie in the discovery of a hierarchy of norms or rules which culminated in one or several points, the moral principles, and in which the lower levels would be explained or "justified" by the higher. To the question, "Why is this act moral?" the explanation can be given, "Because it falls under these definite rules"; and if one asks further, "Why are all the acts falling under this rule moral?" this would be explained by saying, "Because they all fall under that next higher rule." And only with the highest norm—with the moral principle or moral principles—is the knowledge of the validating grounds, a justification, no longer possible in this way. There ethics is at an end for him who sees it as a mere normative science.

8. *Ethics as a "Normative Science"*

We now see clearly what meaning the phrase "normative science" can have, and in what sense alone ethics can "justify" an act or its valuation. In modern philosophy since Kant, the idea repeatedly appears that ethics as a normative science is something completely different from the "factual sciences." It does not ask, "When is a person judged to be good?" or, "Why is he judged to be good?" These questions concern mere facts and their explanation. But it does ask, "With *what right* is that person judged to be good?" It does not trouble itself with what is actually valued, but asks: "What is valuable? What should be valued?" And here obviously the question is quite different.

But *this* manner of opposing normative and factual sciences is fundamentally false. For if ethics furnishes a justification it does so only in the sense just explained, namely, in a relative-hypothetical way, not absolutely. It "justifies" a certain judgment only to the extent that it shows that the judgment corresponds to a certain norm; that this norm itself is "right," or justified, it can neither show nor, by itself, determine. Ethics must simply recognize this as a fact of human nature. Even as a normative science, a science can do no more than *explain;* it can never set up or establish a norm

(which alone would be equivalent to an absolute justification). It is never able to do more than to discover the rules of the judgment, to read them from the
facts before it; the origin of norms always lies outside
and before science and knowledge. This means that
their origin can only be apprehended by the science,
and does not lie within it. In other words: if, or in so
far as, the philosopher answers the question "What is
good?" by an exhibition of norms, this means only that
he tells us what "good" *actually* means; he can never
tell us what good *must* or *should* mean. The question
regarding the validity of a valuation amounts to asking
for a higher acknowledged norm under which the
value falls, and this is a question of *fact*. The question of the justification of the highest norms or the
ultimate values is senseless, because there is nothing
higher to which these could be referred. Since modern ethics, as we remarked, often speaks of this absolute justification as *the* fundamental problem of ethics,
it must be said, unfortunately, that the formulation of
the question from which it proceeds is simply meaningless.

The perversity of such a formulation of the question
will be exhibited by a famous example. John Stuart
Mill has often been justly criticized because he thought
himself able to deduce from the fact that a thing was
desired that it was in itself *desirable*. The double
meaning of the word desirable ("capable of being desired" and "worth desiring") misled him. But his
critics were also wrong, for they rested their criticism

upon the same false presupposition (expressly formulated by neither), namely, that the phrase "in itself desirable" had a definite meaning (by "in itself" I mean "for its own sake," not merely as a means to an end); but in fact they could give it no meaning. If I say of a thing that it is desirable, and mean that one must desire it as a means if one desires a certain end, then everything is perfectly clear. If, however, I assert that a thing is desirable simply in itself, I cannot say what I mean by this statement; it is not verifiable and is therefore meaningless. A thing can be desirable only with respect to something else, not in itself. Mill believed himself able to deduce what is in itself desirable from what actually is desired; his opponents held that these had nothing to do with one another. But ultimately neither side knew what it said, for both failed to give an absolute meaning to the word "desirable." The question whether something is desirable for its own sake is no question at all, but mere empty words. On the other hand, the question of what actually is desired for its own sake is of course quite sensible, and ethics is actually concerned only with answering this question. Mill succeeded in arriving at this real question, in the passage criticized, and thus freed himself of the senseless form of the question, to be sure, less by his false argument than by his healthy instinct, while his opponents remained tied to it and continued to search for an absolute justification of desire.

9. *Ethics as Factual Science*

Such norms as are recognized as the ultimate norms, or highest values, must be derived from human nature and life as facts. Therefore, no result of ethics can stand in contradiction to life; ethics cannot declare as evil or false those values which lie at the foundation of life; its norms cannot demand or command anything that is in a real opposition to those final norms recognized by life. Where such opposition occurs it is a sure sign that the philosopher has misunderstood his problem, and has failed to solve it; that he has unwittingly become a moralist, that he feels uncomfortable in the role of a knower and would prefer to be a creator of moral values. The demands and claims of a morally creative person are merely subjects for investigation for the philosopher, mere objects for cognitive consideration; and this holds also if he should by chance, at other times, be this creative man himself.

We just said that there could be no real opposition between the meaning of the word "good" that is actually accepted in life, and the meaning found by the philosopher. An *apparent* difference can of course occur, for language and thought are very imperfect in daily life. Often the speaker and valuer is himself not clear as to what he expresses, and often his valuations rest on a false interpretation of the facts, and would at once change with a correction of the mistake. The philosopher would have the task of discovering such errors and faulty expressions, and would have to recognize the true norms that lie at the root of moral judgments, and place them in opposition to the apparent ones which the agent, or valuer, believes himself to follow. And in so doing he would, perhaps, find it necessary to delve deep into the human soul. Always, however, it would be an actual, already fundamental norm that he would find there.

The ultimate valuations are facts existing in human consciousness, and even if ethics were a normative science it would not cease because of this to be a science of *facts*. Ethics has to do entirely with the *actual;* this seems to me to be the most important of the propositions which determine its task. Foreign to us is the pride of those philosophers who hold the questions of ethics to be the most noble and elevated of questions just because they do not refer to the common *is* but concern the pure *ought*.

Of course, after one is in the possession of such a system of norms, of a system of applications of the concepts good and evil, one can consider the connections of the members of the hierarchy, the order of the individual rules, quite independently of any relation to actuality; one can investigate merely the inner structure of the system. And this holds even if the norms are not the really valid ones, but are falsely considered such, or are freely imagined and arbitrarily established. The last case would indeed possess only the interest of a game and would make no claim to the name of "ethics." Ethics as a normative science would, however, furnish a hierarchical order of rules, in which all acts and attitudes and characters would possess a definite place with respect to their moral value. And of course this would be true not only of existing acts and attitudes, but also of all possible ones; for if the system is to be of any value it must beforehand supply a place for every possibility of human behavior. After becoming acquainted with the highest norms, one can consider the whole system without any reference to actual behavior, by merely considering the possible. Thus Kant emphasized that for his moral philosophy it was indifferent whether or not any moral will actually existed. Hence ethics conceived as a theory of norms would exhibit the characteristics of an "ideal science"; it would have to do with a system of ideal rules, which could, of course, be applied to actuality, and would only thereby possess any interest, but the rules would have meaning quite independently of this application, and could be investigated in their relations to one another. Thus someone might have invented the rules of chess, and might have considered their application to the individual matches even if the game had never been played, except in his mind, between imaginary opponents.

10. *Ethics Seeks Causal Explanation*

To recapitulate: We began with the position that the task of ethics is to "explain the moral good," and we asked, first, what sort of thing this "good" is which we want to explain. We found that this subject-matter of ethics is not given to us as simply as, say, the subject-matter of optics, light, that is, by a mere sensation; but that for its determination the discovery of a "moral principle" or a whole system of principles or rules is necessary. If we call a discipline that concerns itself with such a system a "normative science," we see that this theory of norms affords nothing more than the discovery of the meaning of the concept "good." In this it exhausts itself. There is no question in it of a real explanation of the good. It offers ethics only the object which is to be explained. Therefore we have from the outset rejected the view of those philosophers who consider ethics to be merely a normative science. No, only where the theory of norms ends does ethical explanation begin. The former fails completely to see the important, exciting questions of ethics, or, worse, turns them aside as foreign in essence to ethics; in truth it fails, except through mistakes, to get beyond the mere linguistic result of determining the meanings of the words "good" and "evil."

It does of course also give us a kind of pseudo-explanation, namely, that which we call justification. Explanation always consists of the reduction of what is to be explained to something else, to something more general; and actually the norms are thus referred back to one another, until the highest are reached. These, the moral principles (or *the* moral principle), according to definition, cannot be referred to other ethical *norms,* and cannot therefore be morally justified.

But this does not mean that all further reduction must be impossible. It might be that the *moral* good could be shown to be a special case of a more general kind of good. Actually the word "good" is used in an extra-moral sense (one speaks not only of good men, but also of good riders, good mathematicians, of a good catch, a good machine, and so forth); it is therefore probable that the ethical and the extra-ethical meanings of the word are somehow connected. If the moral good can in this manner be subsumed under a wider concept of the good, then the question, "Why is moral behavior good?" could be answered by, "Because it is good in a more general sense of the word." The highest moral norm would be justified by means of an extra-moral norm; the moral principle would be referred back to a higher principle of life.

Possibly the reduction could go on a few more steps, but the final norm, the highest principle, can in no way be justified, for the very reason that it is the last. It would be senseless to ask for a further justification, a further explanation. It is not the norms, principles, or values themselves that stand in need of and are capable of explanation, but rather the actual facts from which they are abstracted. These facts are the acts of giving rules, of valuation, of approbation in human consciousness; they are thus real events in the life of the soul. "Value," "the good," are mere abstractions, but valuation, approbation, are actual psychic occurrences, and separate acts of this sort are quite capable of explanation, that is, can be reduced to one another.

And here lies the proper task of ethics. Here are the remarkable facts which excite philosophic wonder, and whose explanation has always been the final goal of ethical inquiry. That man actually approves of certain actions, declares certain dispositions to be "good," appears not at all self-explanatory to the philosopher, but often very astonishing, and he therefore asks his "Why?" Now, in all of the natural sciences every explanation can be conceived as a *causal* explanation, a truth which we need not prove here; therefore the "why" has the sense of a question concerning the *cause* of that psychical process in which man makes a valuation, establishes a moral claim. (We must make clear that when we speak of the discovery of the "cause," we mean by the term "cause" only a popular abbreviation for the statement of the complete laws governing the event to be known.)

In other words, the *determination* of the contents of the concepts of good and evil is made by the use of moral principles and a system of norms, and affords a relative justification of the lower moral rules by the higher; scientific *knowledge* of the good, on the other hand, does not concern norms, but refers to the cause, concerns not the justification but the explanation of moral judgments. The theory of norms asks, *"What* does actually serve as the standard of conduct?" Explanatory ethics, however, asks *"Why* does it serve as the standard of conduct?"

11. *Formulation of the Fundamental Question*

It is clear that in essence the first question is a dry,
formal matter that could win little interest from man
did it not have such importance for practice, and if the
path to its answer did not offer so many opportunities
for profound insight into human nature. The second
question, however, leads directly to these profundities.
It concerns the real grounds, the actual causes and
motives that drive one to distinguish between good
and evil, and call forth the acts of moral judgment.
Not only judgments, but also *conduct,* for this follows
upon judgment. The explanation of moral judgment
cannot be separated from the explanation of conduct.
To be sure, one should not believe, without further
reason, that everyone arranges his conduct according
to his moral judgments. Obviously, that would be a
false assumption. The connection, although indissol-
uble, is more complicated. What a man values, approves, and desires is finally inferred from his actions
—better from these than from his assertions, though
these, too, are kinds of action. What kind of demands
one makes of himself and others can only be known
from one's conduct. A man's valuations must somehow appear among the motives of his acts; they cannot,
in any case, be discovered anywhere else. He who
traces the causes of conduct far enough must come
upon the causes of all approbation. The question of
the causes of conduct is, therefore, more general than

that of the grounds of moral judgments; its answer
would give more comprehensive knowledge, and it
would be methodologically profitable to start with it
even if it were not necessary to begin with the study
of conduct as the only thing observable.

Therefore, we may and should replace the question
raised above, "What motives cause us to establish moral
norms?" by the other question, "What are the motives
of conduct in general?"   (We formulate the question
in this general way and do not at once restrict it to
moral actions because, according to what has been said,
it might be possible to deduce valuations and their
motives just as well, if not better, from immoral or
neutral acts.)   We are the more warranted in relating
our question at once to *conduct,* since man interests
himself in valuations only because conduct depends
upon them.   If moral approbation were something that
remained enclosed in the depths of the heart, if it could
never appear in any way and could not exert the least
influence on the life, happiness and unhappiness of
man, no one would bother himself with it, and the
philosopher would become acquainted with this unimportant phenomenon only by an act of introspec-
tion.   That wonder concerning the moral judgments
of man, which we have described as the earliest impulse
leading to the formulation of ethical questions, is above
all wonder at his own actual moral behavior.

Therefore, we inquire into the causes, that is, the
regularity and order, of all human actions, with the
aim of discovering the motives of moral actions.   And

we profit in so doing because we can postpone the
question regarding the essence of morality, the moral
principle, until we solve the problem of the natural
law governing behavior in general. When, however,
we come to know about action in general, it will certainly be much easier to learn what is peculiar to moral
actions and to define the content of the concept "good"
without difficulty. Perhaps it will turn out that we no
longer feel the necessity of determining a sharp bound-
ary for it (just as, after the physical explanation of
light, the question of how and whether the concept of
"light" is to be distinguished from that of heat radiation or ultra-violet radiation loses all interest).

12. *The Method of Ethics Is Psychological*

Thus the central problem of ethics concerns the
causal explanation of moral behavior; all others in
relation to it sink to the level of preliminary or subor-
dinate questions. The moral problem was most clearly
formulated in this way by Schopenhauer, whose sound
sense of reality led him to the correct path here (if not
in the solution) and guarded him from the Kantian
formulation of the problem and from the post-Kantian
philosophy of value.

The problem which we must put at the center of
ethics is a purely psychological one. For, without
doubt, the discovery of the motives or laws of any kind
of behavior, and therefore of moral behavior, is a purely

psychological affair. Only the empirical science of the laws which describe the life of the soul can solve this problem. One might wish to derive from this a supposedly profound and destructive objection to our formulation of the problem. For, one might say, "In such case there would be no ethics at all; what is called ethics would be nothing but a part of psychology!" I answer, "Why shouldn't ethics be a part of psychology?" Perhaps in order that the philosopher have his science for himself and govern autonomously in this sphere? He would, indeed, thereby be freed of many burdensome protests of psychology. If he laid down a command, *"Thus* shall man act," he would not have to pay attention to the psychologist who said to him, "But man *cannot* act so, because it contradicts psychological laws!" I fear greatly that here and there this motive, though hidden, is at work. However, if one says candidly that "there is no ethics," because it is not necessary to label a part of psychology by a special name, then the question is merely terminological.

It is a poor recommendation of the philosophical spirit of our age that we so often attempt to draw strict lines of division between the sciences, to separate ever new disciplines, and to prove their autonomy. The true philosopher goes in the opposite direction; he does not wish to make the single sciences self-sufficient and independent, but, on the contrary, to unify and bring them together; he wishes to show that what is common to them is what is most essential, and that what is different is accidental and to be viewed as belonging to practical methodology. *Sub specie aeternitatis* there is for him only *one* reality and *one* science.

Therefore, if we decide that the fundamental question of ethics, "Why does man act morally?" can be answered only by psychology, we see in this no degradation of, nor injury to, science, but a happy simplification of the world-picture. In ethics we do not seek independence, but only the truth.

CHAPTER II

What Are the Motives of Human Conduct?

1. *Activity and Conduct*

As we learn from experience, not every human action allows of moral judgment; the greater part of our lives is filled with activities which, considered in themselves, are beyond good and evil. All our daily activities, work and play, necessities as well as amusements, are formed of a vast number of complicated movements which may be executed well or poorly, but which cannot be called "good" or "evil." How we place our feet when walking, hold a pen when writing, or move our fingers in piano-playing is, from the ethical point of view, perfectly indifferent. The exceptions in which activities of this sort are subjected to moral judgment are easily shown to be merely apparent. If, for example, a pianist pains his audience because of clumsy finger movements, his errors are, under certain conditions, morally disapproved; but closer examination shows that the judgment refers not to the activity of the hands themselves, but only to the prior resolution to appear before the public with insufficient technique.

31

This holds in general. Ethics has to do only with "resolutions." Certain acts against which the stream of activity breaks stand out in the regular flow of activity that fills our existence (and is morally irrelevant). These acts represent the decisions of life; they alone deserve the name of "conduct"; all else is mere "activity."

How is conduct distinguished from mere activity? To begin with, the personality is much more implicated in conduct; it rises from greater depths, while activity is external, more superficial, and often fails to come to the light of consciousness. But the difference must be more sharply drawn. Psychology offers us a means of doing this, since it applies to genuine conduct the significant title of "acts of will." In mere activity no act of will or decision occurs. Such activity occurs as immediate, although not necessarily unconscious, reactions to definite stimuli. In playing the piano the perception of written notes calls forth the corresponding finger movement without any intervening act of will. The player does not continuously decide, "Now I shall move this finger, now that, and now my arm," and so forth. The action proceeds according to the "ideo-motor" pattern, that is, an idea or a perception or some sensation functions directly as a stimulus; or, speaking psychologically, a stimulus of the sensory centers of the nervous system flows directly into the motor centers and brings forth the corresponding movement without delay.

2. *The Nature of the Act of Will*

This is the normal course of all our acts. It would never be disturbed, our whole life would run color-lessly on in mere activity, and there would be no acts of will, if at any time only *one* stimulus were at work. In such a case we would never have formed the con-cept of "will," we would have had no occasion for, or possibility of, doing so. What we call an act of will occurs only where several stimuli are at work simul-taneously, to which one cannot respond at the same time, because they lead to incompatible activities. What happens in such a case of "conflicting motives?" In general, the following: there occurs a peculiar oscil-lation of events of consciousness, namely, a more or less rapid shift of ideas, which alternately appear and dis-appear, as weaker and stronger, clearer and more confused. They are the imaginative pictures of the results of the different activities aroused by the stimuli, which in this manner attempt, so to speak, to triumph over one another, dispute the possession of the field of attention, and mutually *inhibit* one another.

Let us consider a very simple case. I decide to leave the room. I go to the door and press the latch. All this occurs automatically; the walking, the movement of my arm and hand, proceed without any act of will being necessary. Now I press the latch and pull on the door—but it does not open! The usual course of events is disturbed. While hitherto, perhaps, I have been thinking of very different matters, now my attention is centered upon the door. I shake it vigorously, sense the tightening of my muscles, and experience exertion against what opposes me. The idea of opening the door stands firmly and clearly before me as an image of my goal. I "will" to open the door.

I believe that the specific experience of "willing" in the whole affair is nothing but the "feeling of exertion" (whether this is simply a feeling of tenseness in the muscles or some special "innervation-sensation" does not concern us here). If the door offers opposition for a long time, the question occurs to me, shall I not desist, and wait until the perhaps inadvertently closed door is opened, or shall I rather seek another exit from the room? In this way the outer inhibition leads to an inner one; the conflict between the end-in-view and the perceived state of affairs turns into a conflict between ideas, between that of exit by force, and that of remaining, or of leaving by the window. These ideas oppose each other; one will triumph, and this triumph is obviously a "decision," an "act of will."

In any act of will we find a struggle against an inner or outer check, which ends with triumph or surrender. For ethics, only the case of inner checks is of any importance; therefore we restrict ourselves to the investigation of those acts of will in which a definite idea (motive, or end-in-view) is in conflict with another or several, and which finally dominates it or them, that is, actually leads to overt activity.

3. *The Concept of Will*

We are accustomed, under the circumstances just described, to speak of an "act of choice," and to say that the person has *chosen* between different possibilities, that he has come to a definite *decision;* and a primitive psychology under the influence of the idea of *substance* treats the matter as if the choice or decision in the conflict of motives were made by a special power, the "will," which, watching the struggle from without, intervenes and bestows the prize of victory upon one or the other of the contestants. But we have nothing to do with such uncritical thinking. Experience fails to disclose any such substratum which stands behind the appearances, and its hypothetical assumption contributes nothing at all to the comprehension of the matter. It leads rather, among other things, to an irresolvable circle; for, on the one hand, we say that the "will" decides between the motives, and, on the other hand, we can give no answer to the question, "What determines the will in its decision?" except, "the motives themselves."

No, there is present no "act of will" that, added to the oscillation of the ends-in-view, and the final triumph of one of them, decides which shall triumph; but the whole process that we have described is itself the act of will. To which, again, we add the conjecture that what is specific and striking in the whole experience may lie in a particular kind of innervation or sensation of tenseness in the muscles.[1] It is well known that the latter is present also when the agent has to overcome a purely inner check or restraint, such as the rejection of certain ends-in-view. The body musculature strains (the hands clench, the face takes on a "determined expression") and the characteristic feeling of exertion, of overcoming, is present.

4. *The Law of Motivation*

Be that as it may, the question which here concerns us as philosophers is, "What determines whether a certain idea triumphs or succumbs in the conflict of motives? What properties distinguish the prevailing motive?" Or, in a more appropriate formulation, "Under what conditions does a definite idea gain the upper hand?" The answer to this question tells us why a man does this rather than that, why in general he prefers something, "wills" something. It is the answer to the question, "What are the motives of human conduct?"

---

[1] For this assumption the following surprising experiment furnishes clear evidence. If one stands sideways with his shoulder against a wall, his arm hanging vertically alongside his body, and presses for some time very strongly against the wall with his arm, as if he were trying to lift it to the horizontal position, which the wall prevents, and then suddenly steps away from the wall, his arm rises at once as if "of its own self" into the horizontal position, without any decision of the will. The cause of this is that the effort of raising the arm is now so small in comparison with the immediately preceding effort that it fails to register in consciousness.

In many, indeed most, situations of life the answer is easy to find; it lies so clearly at hand that it can be correctly given without further trouble by any un- prejudiced judge, that is, by any man not led astray by philosophizing and moralizing. Such a person will tell us that, at least in general, in a conflict of several ends-in-view, a man will act in the direction of the *most pleasant.*

What does this statement mean?

Every idea, every content of our consciousness, as we learn from experience, possesses a certain *tone.* And this has the consequence that the content in question is not something completely neutral, or indifferent, but is somehow characterized as agreeable or disagreeable, attractive or repellent, joyful or painful, pleasant or unpleasant. We adopt the last mentioned terminology and say, every experience has an emotional tone that is pleasant or unpleasant, or, in the substantival language of psychology, in every experience there is a feeling of pleasure or of pain. The essence of these feelings is of course indescribable—every simple experience is beyond all description—and one can only make clear what is meant by appropriate indications. Here we should note that we use the words "pleasant" and "unpleasant" in the widest possible sense. All further questions, such as whether there are different kinds of pleasantness and unpleasantness, or only different grades, we put aside; most of them, like the one just mentioned, seem to me to be improperly formulated. Of course, I have very different experiences when I stroke soft silk, when I attend a performance of *Midsummer Night's Dream,* when I admire an heroic act, when the proximity of a beloved person makes me happy; but in a certain respect there is undoubtedly a similarity in the mental dispositions in all these cases, and we express this when we say that all of them have *pleasant* emotional tones, or that all of them are *joyful.* On the other hand, however different my feelings may be when I cut my finger, when I hear a violinist play a false note, when I think of the injustice of the world, when I stand at the bier of a friend, there is some kind of similarity in all these cases which still justifies me in considering them all as belonging to a single class, and in saying they are *unpleasant* feelings.

The enumeration of these examples should not be misunderstood. In exceptional cases it may very well be that the last mentioned situations are pleasant, and those mentioned first unpleasant. Sensations of bodily pain can be pleasant (perversion), false violin tones can amuse and please me (as in the case of intended comedy), indeed, a pessimistic philosopher can even be pleased with the injustice of the world, viewing it triumphantly as a confirmation of his views: "I told you so!" No definite emotional tone belongs to a specific experience as such; it depends upon the whole situation, just as a white object can appear in any color, depending upon the lighting.

After these explanations we can state that the decision of the will proceeds in the direction of the most pleasant end-in-view, in the following manner: of the

ideas which function as motives, that one gains the
upper hand which finally possesses the highest degree
of pleasant emotional tone, or the least unpleasant tone,
and thus the act in question is unambiguously determined.

Two remarks must be introduced here. First, the
decision occurs only after the difference in emotional
tone reaches a certain point, because without this
assumption it is obvious that no oscillation in "choice"
could ever occur. The second remark is that when I
describe the conflict of motives as an opposition of
ideas, this is to be considered as a way of speaking only,
and not as anything binding or compromising. Perhaps other psychic acts are involved, but this question
can remain undecided for our purposes.

Before we discuss the validity of the above proposition, we must devote a moment to the difficulties which
lie hidden in the notion of "most pleasant," or "least
unpleasant." The use of these phrases obviously presupposes that one can compare the different pleasant
and unpleasant situations, and can speak of more or
less with respect to feelings. However, this seems to
be impossible, because the intensity of feelings (or any
other psychical state) certainly cannot actually be
measured, cannot be determined quantitatively. This
is doubtless true; a calculus of pleasure and pain with
sums and differences of feelings would be meaningless.
Still, we can carry through the comparison of ideas
with respect to their "pleasure value" or their "motiva-
tive power," which is necessary for the understanding

of acts of will. This follows from the fact that in every-day life we constantly say with sense and understanding, "I prefer this to that, but not as much as I like the other," and so forth. It seems to me that the matter sums up as follows: When two ends-in-view, *a* and *b,* appear alternately before one, they are not directly balanced one against the other; but we find that, for example, the transition from *a* to *b* is an unpleasant experience, while the transition from *b* to *a* is pleasant. Thus we are able to say, by way of definition, that *a* with respect to *b* is the more pleasant or the less unpleasant idea. In general, we must not consider the genesis of acts of will as a static balancing, but rather as a dynamic process, a flux, in which the waxing and waning and shifting of the images is at least as much tinged with feeling as are the images themselves. Thus we see how one can speak sensibly of more or less with respect to pleasure and pain, without actually presupposing quantitative differences. We require nothing more than the opposition of pleasure and pain in the transition from one idea to another. Among a number of motives present the most attractive or least unattractive end-in-view is distinguished by the fact that every departure from it to any one of the others is joined with an inhibiting pain. Thus it represents a summit, appears as such in the center of consciousness, and draws conduct toward itself.

5. *In Proof of the Law of Motivation*

Having thus become clear regarding the *meaning* of
the law, that in the conflict of motives the decision goes
to the most pleasant or least unpleasant, we turn now
to the question of its *validity*.

I have already remarked that, for the majority of
cases of every-day acts of will, its validity is indispu-
table and obvious. When a child reaches for the largest
of several cakes offered it, when I take a walk in the
open air instead of going to a faculty meeting, when I
reflect whether the destination of a summer's trip shall
be the sea or the mountains, when one wavers between
a visit to the opera or to a concert, between buying
black or brown shoes—then, normally, in all these
cases and in a thousand similar ones, there is not the
shadow of a doubt that the decision is determined by
the agreeableness or disagreeableness, by the pleasure
quality of the end-in-view, and that it takes place in the
described way.

But in order to pursue the study of ethics, indeed to
understand the mechanism of conduct at all, we are
little served by a rule that holds good in the majority
of cases only; we need a *law,* that is, a description of
relationships that fits *all* cases. Now the familiar
method always used by science is to ask whether a rule
verified in many cases may not itself be a law, that is,
actually hold for *all* cases. At any rate, one begins
with this assumption and often finds it verified, in that

all cases which at first sight seem not to fit the rule are apparent exceptions only, their actual subsumption under the law being hidden by complicated circumstances.

Applying this method to our problem, we express the provisional assumption that the rule governing many cases of motivation may itself be a law, that is, we examine whether or not in *every* case of an act of will the decision be not determined in the direction of the most pleasant, or least unpleasant, motive.

6. *The Law of Motivation in the Case of Sacrifice*

At first sight this seems not to be the case at all. It happens that a well-bred child chooses the smallest cake, even though it obviously would "rather have" the largest; and do we not very often find ourselves in the situation of the child and trudge toward a painful, unpleasant goal? Does this not happen whenever we "make a sacrifice?" The fact is, many, if not most, philosophers believe that in such situations the prevailing motive is certainly not the most pleasant, and is often extremely unpleasant. Therefore, they do not consider the law to be universally valid; they deny it represents the law of motivation, and say it is not at all true that a man can desire only that the idea of which possesses relatively greater pleasure for him. They hold that he can desire simply anything, and many of them (including Kant) are of the opinion that although human conduct is determined by pleasant or unpleasant feelings in the described manner in all other cases, this is simply not so in the case of *moral acts*. The latter, according to them, form an exception and are, indeed, defined and distinguished by this fact. Hence we see the extent and importance of our problem, and we cannot be content before learning whether our law of motivation holds only in the limited sphere of the trivial acts of every-day life, or whether it is a true law governing every act of will without exception.

Let us not hesitate to analyze more closely the case of the child who has to choose between its several cakes. If the child takes the smallest in order to leave the larger ones for its companions, one may well consider this to be a "moral" act. Can its behavior really not be explained in terms of the law that the most pleasant end-in-view determines the will? I believe that we must admit that this is very easily done. For how is the state of mind of this child distinguished from that of the other who thoughtlessly takes the largest? We said before that even the child who here decides to make a "sacrifice" would "rather have" a larger piece of cake than a smaller one. But what is the significance of this? Obviously, that under otherwise similar conditions the idea of the larger cake is more pleasant (in the sense previously defined) than is that of the smaller. But conditions here are not the same, since in the mind of the child who renounces, because of his education or natural propensities, certain events are happening which are absent in the other child; and these act so that the original emotional tone of the conflicting ends-in-view is entirely altered. They are events of association by means of which there enter, more or less clearly, into consciousness ideas of pleased or displeased parents, their words of praise or censure, or the ideas of happy or disappointed companions. The strong emotional tones that belong to all these ideas are transmitted to the motive with which they are associated, and completely modify its initial pleasure value. The image of a larger piece of cake is indeed more pleasant than that of a smaller one if both stand side by side unaccompanied by other ideas, but here each is joined by a complex of other ideas together with their feelings, and these feelings are transferred, as experience shows, to those images, even when the ideas to which they originally belonged no longer appear in consciousness. By this process the idea of the lesser good can easily become more pleasant than that of the greater, and the apparently paradoxical decision occurs in complete conformity with our law of motivation. Every one admits that the act of will could take place as it did only because of certain external influences, for no one believes that a child can choose the smaller cake *merely* because it likes the larger one more. And pedagogical experience teaches us that these influences are of the sort described. Since this suffices to explain the fact completely, we need no further hypothesis. Thus our law of motivation has here been entirely verified; and it is verified in all other cases we may choose to consider. Having dealt with a very simple example, we do well now to turn our attention to those acts of will

in which the very highest matters are at stake, and
which have from olden times been drawn into the foreground of ethical inquiries. Such are the cases of
seemingly-greatest renunciation, or self-sacrifice.

7. *The Law of Motivation in the Case of Heroism*

The idea of personal destruction is, in general, one of
the most terrifying; not the most terrifying, for there
are enough miseries in comparison with which death
is felt as a soothing relief. Yet we observe, in life and
history, acts of will whose fatal and miserable consequences are not only inevitable for the performer, but
are clearly seen by him to be involved as the goal of his
action. The martyr accepts pain and death for the
sake of an idea, a friend gives his life or "happiness"
for his friend. Can any one in earnest say of such
persons that their decisions are determined by the motives which possess the most pleasant or the least unpleasant emotional tones?

According to my firm conviction, one cannot say
anything else if one would tell the truth, for such are
the facts. Let us then try to analyze and understand
the motive of heroism. The hero acts "for the sake of
a cause"; he desires to carry out an idea or realize a
definite goal. It is clear that the thought of this goal
or that idea dominates his consciousness to such an
extent that there is in it hardly room for any other
thoughts. At least this holds in the case of inspiration,

from which alone an heroic act can arise. It is true that the idea of his own painful destruction is present, but, however burdened with pain it may be in itself, it is inhibited and repressed by the predominant end-in-view, which finally triumphs in an "act of will," in an effort which becomes stronger and sharper the longer and more clearly the thought of the unavoidable catastrophe confronts him. What is the source of the astonishing force of the decisive end-in-view? Whence the power of this affect? Without doubt this is due to *emotion*. Inspiration is the greatest pleasure that can fall to the lot of man. To be inspired by something means to be overcome by the greatest joy in the thought of it. The man who, under the stress of inspiration, decides to help a friend or save another creature from pain and destruction, whatever the cost, finds the thought of this act so profoundly joyful, so overwhelmingly pleasant that, at the moment, the idea of the preservation of his own life and the avoidance of pain cannot compare with it. And he who fights for a cause with such inspiration that he accepts all persecution and insult realizes his idea with such elevated pure joy that neither the thought of his miseries nor their actual pain can prevail aught against it. The notion of giving up his purpose because of pain is, for him, more unpleasant than the pain itself.

Thus the correctness of our law of the will is shown in even the most extreme case, and quite naturally, without any auxiliary hypothesis. It is, in fact, universally true that the will follows the motive which has

the greatest degree of pleasant feeling connected with
it.

8. *Rebuttal of False Objections and Explanations*

It was, of course, a gross error to try, as men did on
the basis of a naïve psychology, to explain the action of
the martyr by saying that his behavior is determined
by a hope of reward in another world, beyond; in this
fashion apparently subsuming it under our law of the
will. This explanation may often fit, but certainly not
always, for there have been unbelieving martyrs, concerned only with this world. Indeed, it does not hold
even in the majority of cases, even though Schiller has
the Maid of Orleans die with the words, "The pain is
brief, the joy is everlasting." ["*Kurz ist der Schmerz,
und ewig ist die Freude.*"]

No, it is not at all necessary that the prevailing
pleasant idea be of one's personal condition. Why
should this be assumed? Perhaps because one believes
that, in general, only ideas of one's own condition can
be pleasant, or, at least, that only such ideas can be
intensely pleasant? This would be a gross misunderstanding of the psychological fact, for the commonest
experiences teach us the opposite. They also teach that
a man is not nearly so much concerned with his own
future good and evil as many older ethical systems
would have us believe. For example, one can easily
see this in the way a man harms himself by being im-
moderate. When he squanders his future happiness

for a mess of pottage, why should he not risk it for the sake of the joy given him in saving some unfortunate?

If we are not clear in this, we run the danger of establishing our law of motivation in an erroneous manner, and hence missing its truth. In fact, such mistaken notions at this point are to blame for the fact that many hold our law to be false. They suppose it to be absurd to say that the martyr suffers and dies because of "pleasure," since in this way one seems to wipe out, either in fact or at least terminologically, all difference between the pleasant and the unpleasant.

When it comes to the confusion of the facts I believe that our representation has avoided just that to which our opponents have fallen victim. It is not a confusion, but on the contrary a finer distinction, if we emphasize that an ordinarily painful experience can, under special conditions, become pleasant, and vice versa. It is this fact that is overlooked by the opponents of our view when they say that a man can act in the direction of any end-in-view, and not only toward a pleasant one. To be sure, any end can be desired, but this does not mean that it has nothing to do with the pleasure tone of the end-in-view, but only that any end can become pleasant. It is as if one said, "Whoever is not blind can see any visible thing." Of course, but only if it be illuminated!

The will can no more direct itself toward an end, the idea of which is simply unpleasant and has absolutely nothing attractive, alluring, or noble in it, than the eye can see an object clothed in utter darkness. In ethical considerations we often come upon the assertion that

man can desire that which is in every respect painful
and unenjoyable to him; but all examples that can be
offered of such a desire show upon analysis that the
end is imagined as in some way still something noble,
great, necessary, propitiative, or valued, no matter how
much woe may be connected with it. As soon as one
succeeds (which is not so easy) in imagining an end
that appears to be *completely* unpleasant, repulsive,
disgusting, bringing suffering, and hateful without
compensation, without any possibility of transfigura-
tion, exhaltation or admiration, then one sees at once
with complete certainty that such an end *cannot* be
desired. It is an inescapable law that the absolutely
repulsive and unpleasant is not a possible object of
desire. Martyrs are of course often fanatics, and a
fanatic often inclines toward perversion; hence bodily
pain can then be pleasant for him. But this case is
very rare, although it frequently happens that the *idea*
of an ordinarily painful state is a joyful one for him.

With this we arrive at a second factual distinction,
which is frequently neglected by those who deny our
law of the will. It is the distinction between the
pleasant idea of a state and the *idea of a pleasant state.*
That is, one can imagine only a thing, a state, or an
event, but not the pleasure connected with the things;
whether the idea itself is joyful or painful does not at
all depend on whether the imagined things, when they
are actually present, have pleasant or unpleasant consequences. As is well known, Dante thought that
there was no greater pain than that connected with

the idea of a pleasant state—if this lay in the past, *Nessun maggior dolore* . . . Our law is concerned only with whether an idea is pleasant, and not with whether it is the idea of something pleasant.

Regarding the objection, often raised, that the law of motivation can be maintained only by a trick of terminology, since one extends the concept of pleasure too widely and designates very different things by the one word, we must say that the real reason for our usage, in grouping together everything which is pleasant or satisfying, lies in the facts. The usage is perfectly natural, and is subsequently justified because it leads to a simple formulation of a fundamental law. And how else would one define the concept of pleasure? The objection raised above cannot be considered a serious one. Of course, we could agree to call only the satisfaction of hunger, thirst, and the sexual impulse "pleasure"—which, perhaps, certain moralists would prefer—but in so doing we should merely satisfy certain prejudices, and it would be necessary to give up the adequate formulation of the law of motivation.

No serious danger, then, threatens our law from this quarter; and one actually finds the conviction of its validity very widespread. Even many philosophers who explicitly oppose it, implicitly presuppose its validity. The institutions of human society all show the universal belief in the validity of the law. For no religion, no system of education, no public institution knows any other means of influencing human action than to strive to make the idea of the end whose realization is desired as pleasant as possible, and the idea of the undesired unpleasant. The clumsiest means of doing this is the promise of reward and the threat of punishment, but there are also more refined, indirect means.

9. *The Law of Motivation Is Not Tautologous*

Such being the case, it is unnecessary to defend the truth of the law of motivation any further; we even find it considered almost self-evident. But we must again be careful not to consider it too self-evident, which is indeed often done. Some think the law says nothing whatever, others that for ethics, at least, it has no significance. We shall begin by examining the first opinion.

We often hear it said that if a man decides in favor of something it is clear that he "prefers" it to something else, that he considers it in some sense better. But this holds only because "to prefer" and "to consider better" are different expressions of the same fact. Our "law" has therefore (it is said) no factual content; it is merely an analytical proposition, a tautology, and affords us no knowledge.

But this argument is false. It rests upon a confusion of "to desire" and "to will." The expressions "to consider better," "to find more satisfying," "to imagine with pleasure," and similar ones, may be treated as synonyms of "to desire." John Stuart Mill saw this clearly when he wrote that to find something pleasing and to desire it are only different ways of expressing the same fact. But "to will" is something else, something more. No reaction need follow mere desire, but volition is inseparably joined to action and conduct; volition is *identical* with the primary, inner stage of conduct, the exertion, the innervation. (Whether this actually leads to bodily motion and to further external effects depends upon external circumstances and can no longer be attributed to him who wills, to the self.) That something imagined with the maximum amount of pleasure is actually willed, that is, leads to innervation, is anything but self-evident; it is simply a fact of experience. We are so accustomed to this fact that we are inclined to believe it is part of the very concept of the willed that it be also something desired. However, we see that here we are concerned with an empirical fact, with a law established by experience; because we can very well imagine a different state of affairs. The child with the piece of cake could, for example, very well observe the larger piece with much greater pleasure and still make the discovery that whenever a smaller or less tasty piece was offered its hand always reached for the latter. And it could be so universally: whenever several ends-in-view of different pleasure values compete with one another the reaction might unhesitatingly proceed in the direction of the least pleasant. This is quite *conceivable*. That man always *wills* what he least *desires* would be a possible law of the will. Of course, under such circumstances, if the world remained as it now is, an individual subject to this law would be destroyed in a very short time. Our actual law of motivation would appear to be a tautology if one defined as the most pleasant idea that which actually leads to conduct; but this is certainly not relevant, since we have assumed from the beginning that by pleasure is meant an indefinable quality immediately known to everyone and different from pain. Only observation can determine that those ideas are the deciding motives which are most richly endowed with this quality; it is not self-evident.

10. *The Law Expresses Significant Knowledge*

A word now concerning the attempt, mentioned above, to show our law of the will to be insignificant. It may be admitted, one says, that man can will only what appears in some way attractive to him. But what of that? The noble man will find the good pleasing, and will do it, while the scoundrel will prefer evil, both according to the same law; and consequently we shall learn nothing regarding the difference between good and evil, concerning the distinction between moral and other conduct. This distinction and everything that ethics is interested in could remain the same even if some other law of the will were true; knowledge of the law leaves us no wiser than we were before concerning ethical matters.

We answer that of course we learn nothing positive concerning what is unique in moral volition, but we learn at least something negative, namely, that the peculiarity of good conduct does not consist in the fact that the pleasure and pain of the agent have nothing to do with his motivation. And, since this has often been maintained, and indeed from it has been derived the opinion that moral behavior proceeds in the direction opposite to the most pleasant motive (William James says that moral conduct is conduct in the line of greatest resistance), we must consider it an important insight to note that our law holds for every volition without exception, and therefore for moral volition.

But more than this is gained. When one asks, why does *A* behave morally and *B* the opposite? we can now answer: because the idea of a certain end is joined with pleasure for *A,* but with its opposite for *B* (both, of course, taken relative to the pleasure-value of the contrary ways of acting). But, one will say, the question is given no final answer in this way; it is only put off. For now one must ask: why, then, is the same idea pleasant for the one and not for the other? Exactly! The question is only put off, but perhaps to a point at which one can hope to answer it easily! We now know where we have to search. It is necessary to make out the laws of feelings, the rules that govern their growth and decline, according to which they work together and against each other, but above all to understand the process whereby they are joined to ideas. Perhaps psychology already knows these laws. As soon as we are in possession of them we shall be able to refer to their ultimate causes the predispositions of men to a certain way of acting; we shall be in position to understand their differences and their origin, and, finally, to give the means whereby their development can be influenced. We shall, with this, have acquired just that knowledge which ethics seeks.

CHAPTER III

What Is Egoism?

1. *Egoism Is "Immoral"*

Many philosophers have thought that a will determined in the described manner, by the maximum pleasure, must be called *egoistic;* because it is supposed to be egoistic, or selfish, to "seek one's own pleasure." And this holds even of those thinkers, like Spinoza, who had a presentiment of the validity of our law, as well as of those, such as Kant, who denied it. The former merely desired to express a fact, but in so doing gave to the word "egoism" so broad a meaning that it became quite useless; the latter desired to discredit the law of the will. They used the word "egoism" with the uncomplimentary meaning which it has in everyday life; but they did not realize that in *this* sense conduct is certainly not at all egoistic when it occurs in accordance with our law of motivation. For no unbiassed person will call an act egoistic which, for example, arises out of joy in the satisfactions of another person.

There is no doubt that in everyday speech this word is used with the intention of blaming; that is, when someone calls certain conduct egoistic he desires to call

up an unpleasant idea of this conduct. Also there is
no doubt that such condemnation is intended as *moral*
condemnation: the word "egoistic" signifies a concept
subsumed under the concept of the "immoral." Thus
egoism is a subspecies of immorality. By learning
what is meant by egoism we learn in part what is
meant by "immorality," and this gives us a clue to the
meaning of "morality," its opposite. If those philosophers were right who hope to derive all immorality
from "egoism," and who see in it the source of all evil,
then with the discovery of the meaning of the word
the whole question of the nature of the moral would
practically be answered; for it would only be necessary
to separate what is indifferent (if anything of the sort
exists) from what is not egoistic to find the moral in
the remainder.

But, however this may be, in any case the inquiry
concerning the nature of egoism can only consist in
determining the sense in which the word is actually
used. It cannot determine that a certain kind of behavior is "really" egoism, and that nothing else can
bear this name.

2. Egoism and "Personal Welfare"

The most convenient, easiest assertion that a philosopher can make about egoism is that it is an "impulse."
Thus we find Schopenhauer saying that all human
conduct can be explained by the existence of three
"main-springs" of conduct, namely, egoism, malice,

and sympathy. This would be an extremely simple mechanism, and further explanation of the three impulses does appear at first very simple. Egoism (according to Schopenhauer and many others) aims at "one's own welfare"; sympathy aims at "another's welfare" and corresponds to altruism; and malice aims at "harm to others." Thus, according to this teaching, one's own welfare and the welfare or harm of others constitute the three situations possessing human interest. The "satisfaction" of an impulse would consist in the realization of its corresponding situation. Is it not significant that in this list there is no impulse directed toward "one's own harm?"

It is easy to see that in this manner it is impossible to get a definition of egoism, or even to understand the nature of an impulse in general. For one must know first what one's "own welfare" is. Does it not consist in the fact that one's own desires are fulfilled, that is, that one's impulses are satisfied? Consequently, if one is sympathetic, the other's welfare means at the same time the realization of one's own desires; if a man is malicious he is satisfied in knowing the other to suffer, and thereby his own welfare is increased. In other words, an act springing out of malice or sympathy would be just as egoistic as conduct motivated by egoism.

We learn from this paradox that by "welfare" one cannot mean the realization of all personal desires, the satisfaction of all of one's own impulses, without giving up the definition of egoism as the impulse aiming at "personal welfare." One of the two at least must be given up. In fact, both must be abandoned in order to obtain a clear idea that will do justice to the actual use of the word. For if one tries to improve Schopenhauer's thought, retaining his way of looking at the matter, by saying that "welfare" means the realization of all desires *with the exception* of those arising from malice or sympathy, then we must ask: with what right are such different activities as striving for power, knowledge, sexual pleasure, enjoyment of art considered to be expressions of *one* impulse, namely "egoism?" This cannot be justified by linguistic usage, for the desires directed, for example, toward knowledge or aesthetic enjoyment are not usually called egoistic; nor can it be grounded in the facts, for evidently we have here a large variety of different "impulses," and the word "egoism" would only be a collective name for them. It would not be coördinated with the impulses, but would stand, as it were, behind or over them, as an impulse of a higher order. Such an impulse, which aimed at the satisfaction of impulses, would of course be a meaningless notion; and thus we discover the extreme carelessness of the usual formulation of the concept, carelessness that makes it impossible to talk clearly and sensibly concerning this matter.

3. *The Nature of Impulse*

Therefore, before carrying our considerations any further, we must ask what it is we wish to designate

by the term "impulse." Linguistically the word obviously means something that pushes, impels, or thrusts;
and so one generally thinks of a force (a "spring")
which in turn is imagined as analogous to muscular
exertion or work. If, however, one is to make the
nature of an impulse clear, one does well to replace
such images by an abstract formulation. And this
must obviously be: an impulse is a human disposition
by means of which man's desires and volitions are
directed toward a definite goal. This formulation,
which, like every statement about "dispositions," "propensities," or "faculties," says but little, obtains a concrete content if we remember that we already know,
from the preceding chapter, how a definite goal comes
to be desired. This desire consists in the fact that the
idea of the goal is pleasant;[1] thus we may say that an
impulse exists whenever an idea (or perception) is
accompanied by a feeling of pleasure. The disposition
which constitutes the essence of impulse is, then, the
inherited or acquired propensity to react to certain
stimuli with feelings. These can of course be unpleasant feelings, for an impulse can be negative in
nature; an unpleasant idea has the tendency to lead to
a movement of avoidance or flight.

---

[1] I do not think that this definition of desire is too broad.
If one objects: "The sight of the moon is pleasant, but we do
not desire the moon," we should answer: "We do desire the
sight of the moon." And again we must warn against a confusion of desire with volition. What is desired is willed only
if no other stronger desires are present.

We see at once that an impulse need not be an enduring, fixed orientation of the soul; it can be temporary and changeable. Because of a passing disposition an idea can come to possess a certain emotional tone even though in general it possesses quite a different one, or none at all.

An impulse is, like a force, characterized by a certain *direction* and a certain *magnitude*. The former is given by the particular idea (or class of ideas) to which the pleasant or unpleasant feelings are joined, the latter by the *intensity* of the feeling, by which is meant its relative strength in relation to the emotional tones of other alternative ideas. (One should bear in mind what was said in the previous chapter on the comparison of feelings of pleasure.)

Impulses, then, are not to be compared to actual tensions or potential energy. The nervous energy that is spent in every act has its seat, so to speak, in the whole organism, not in an individual impulse; the latter merely determines the path it takes. The "strength" of an impulse only conditions its preponderance over other impulses; the intensity of the act, the power with which it is carried out, depends upon the total energy which is available to the agent. The word "inclination," which Kant always used in place of "impulse," offers less occasion for the confusion of impulse and expanding force, and therefore is the better expression. For an impulse does not actually "impel," but "inclines" or directs a tendency. When we attribute to anyone an inclination toward certain things, conditions, or activities, this is only another way of expressing the fact that the idea of those things or activities is pleasant for him. And since there is hardly any idea, or perception, or any psychic event to which a feeling is not joined, we can say that in every moment of our conscious life some inclination is active: our whole life is a life of impulse. This is the empirical basis upon which rests the notion of many philosophers that the essence of life is the "will." (According to Schopenhauer, it is the essence of the whole universe.)

If we connect what is said above on the nature of "impulse" with the law of the will enunciated in the preceding chapters, we realize the important truth that, no matter what one's conduct is, one always follows some inclination. One can do and will only what one has an impulse to will and do. For the law of the will asserts that one can act only toward that end whose idea is most pleasant for one, and this means in the direction of the strongest impulse. Thus Kant's categorical imperative, which demands that one act wholly independently of one's inclinations, demands what is impossible. It goes contrary to the facts of psychology and therefore has no interest for us. Moral conduct is either impossible or it is derived from natural inclinations.

4. Is Egoism an Impulse?

After making clear the meaning of the term "impulse," the question whether egoism is an impulse obtains a clear meaning, and we can now answer it. If egoism or selfishness were one inclination among others, this would mean that certain definite ideas were pleasant to the egoist which for other men would be unpleasant or without any emotional tone whatever. Which ideas could these be?

Here we must consider the concept of "personal welfare," already touched upon. Is there an idea of "personal welfare?" Obviously there is not, for an idea is always an intuited, given content of consciousness, while "welfare," on the contrary, is something extremely abstract; hence there is no idea of "welfare" in general. If we assign someone the task of imagining his own welfare he cannot carry it out; he can only picture definite situations in which he would say that he is satisfied.

Can we deduce from this that only those inclinations are possible which are directed upon particular imaginable situations or things, that there can be no impulse directed toward the abstraction "personal welfare," and that therefore egoism must be something else? Such a conclusion would be premature, for there are undoubtedly such impulses as the will to power, the will to wealth, and yet power and wealth are wholly abstract, and not directly imaginable.

Shall we say that a general concept such as "power" can also be emotionally colored, like an actual idea, and thereby constitute the nucleus of an impulse? This would be a psychological error that would make us guilty of the rationalization of ethics, from which all systems in the history of philosophy have suffered; instead of investigating the individual cases of actual psychic processes connected with moral feeling they deal at once with abstractions and generalizations which, just because they originate in the thought of everyday life, are to be tested doubly carefully. "Power" in general cannot be pictured by anyone, but only the activities in which it manifests itself. The man who longs for power sees himself carry admiring multitudes before him in a fiery speech, sees how he gives commands to cringing subordinates, how he stands majestically before humbled opponents, and so forth. He who strives for wealth cannot imagine this directly, but pictures the individual things which constitute, represent, or symbolize it: a castle, a park, a steam-yacht, a dollar bill, a table loaded with delicacies, and similar things. The sight and thought of such things are saturated with feelings, as is characteristic for the process of desire. How greatly powerful desire is dependent upon the liveliness and concreteness of the exciting idea or perception is known to all poets (indefinite "yearning" is a very different thing from desire); philosophers should also learn this in order that they might not replace the actual human soul by artificial constructions having nothing to do with real life.

That, despite the psychological facts described, we still may speak of "the" will to wealth, and must do this (for its resolution into an inclination toward bank notes, another toward automobiles, and so forth, would be absurd) rests upon the fact that something is common to all these desired things; namely, their high money-value, and that, conversely, all things possessing this common property are desired by the same individual. This indicates that in all these cases, somehow, a common *cause* can be made responsible for the fact that just *those* objects which belong to the class defined by the common property arouse desire when imagined or perceived by a certain individual. The presence of this common element, or this cause, is now expressed as the presence of an "impulse," and for this reason the referring of the conduct to impulse signifies a kind of explanation or knowledge, for knowledge consists in discovering what is common to different entities.

5. *The Possibility of Imagining "Personal States"*

We are now prepared to answer the question, "Is there an impulse that is directed toward 'personal welfare,' and which therefore may be called egoism?" The question must be answered in the affirmative if there is a special class of objects of desire whose common characteristic consists of the fact that all of them are states of personal welfare; otherwise it must be denied.

In fact we do not succeed in delimiting a class of states in the desired manner. Try it! If one meant— this is the first attempt—by a state of welfare simply any pleasant state, the following would result: we should have to separate out all of the acts of will of an individual in which the prevailing (and therefore relatively pleasant) idea was the idea of a state of the agent himself. From these acts we should have to select again those (for they would not be all) in which the imagined personal state was pleasant; then we should have to say that these last, finally selected acts proceeded from the egoism of the individual.

Both selections meet with insuperable difficulties. The first, which would select the cases in which the idea of a personal state functions as motive, faces the epistemological difficulty of clearly distinguishing the ego from the environment—the difficulty, namely, of deciding whether an idea is really only of a state of oneself, or whether it includes something else, say, the external conditions of the internal state. For example: suppose someone would like to hear the "Eroica" and decides to attend a certain concert. In general, the events proceed so that, as a result perhaps of an announcement of the concert in a newspaper, the person imagines certain sounds and melodies of Beethoven; in addition he imagines the orchestra playing, pictures the conductor, the lighted hall, perhaps musical notes, and so forth; all these ideas or images are very pleasing and in the end lead to action (the purchase of tickets, and so forth). And now suppose someone asserting that the whole process might take place differently, so that the person does not think of the concert hall nor the orchestra nor the conductor nor the tones of the symphony, but only pictures his own state of musical enjoyment. In the first case the impulse to which the action corresponds would be the requirement of or desire for music; in the second it would be egoism!

Such an opposition of the two cases is untenable, for the following reasons: *First* (and this is the most fundamental), it is doubtful whether a case of the second sort is at all possible. I do not believe that it is. I fail to discover how anyone can imagine himself in a state of musical enjoyment without somehow also imagining the conditions and the object (the composition) of his enjoyment. It seems to me that the process must always take place in the manner first described, or similarly, because the state of the self cannot be isolated from the "impressions" which call it forth; for in fact these impressions belong to the state. Every idea presupposes a perception to which it is related as a copy or secondary experience. Since there is no perception of the personal state (but only the state itself, which can also be a perception), it follows that there is no idea of it. One could at best attempt to distinguish the second case from the first, and consider it exceptional, by admitting that in both cases the process is essentially the same, but that in the second is added the thought, "All these events of the musical performance come to my attention as a result of and only in so far as they produce a special condition in me." But what of it? This accompanying thought would be a noteworthy additional fact, a peculiarity of the individual, but no special new "impulse" would be given with it; nothing would be altered in the act of the will. One cannot say, "The man would not have gone to the concert unless he had that thought, and therefore the impulse lay in it," for, according to the presupposition, the musical impulse is already present (because otherwise the concert would fail to produce a pleasant state in him); and if the impulse is present and there are no hindrances, the action must follow even without the accessory thought, and therefore this plays no part in the motivation.

In the second place, suppose that a pure idea of nothing but one's personal state were possible, and occurred sometimes as a motive: this would be a very special orientation of consciousness, it would be an extraordinary case, and therefore cannot constitute the case of "egoism"; for egoism is not at all rare, but an everyday matter. There is no doubt that the thought of one's own states is exceptional, and could occur only in hyperacute, sophisticated men. And it is just as clear that a natural man who thinks very little can be a robust egoist; and therefore that thought cannot be the characteristic property of the egoist. One realizes this most clearly by picturing the disposition of an egotistical person. Suppose that such a person robs his companions of something, and appropriates it all without thinking of the others. Does he not act selfishly in all such cases, or is he selfish only when he continuously pictures to himself, during his violent or cunning procedure, how pleased he will be when he gets the object?

We have restricted our observations to certain examples, but the result holds generally. However hard

one tries, one fails to find a pure idea of a personal
state; and whenever this does seem to occur one sees
at once that there is nothing new in the situation as a
whole, but only a special thought is added. Our
thoughts seem above all to be directed upon ourselves
when we imagine our future bodily state. But this of
course would not be an idea of the "self" at all, but of
something external. Still, apart from this, egoism
could not be so defined; the concept would have, in
comparison with common usage, a far too restricted
scope. He who interested himself in nothing but his
meals would certainly be called an egoist, but he need
never think of his "self"; his soul (if this word is
appropriate to such a man) would be concerned with
nothing but ideas of his favorite food and drink. The
object, not the subjective condition of satisfaction
which its possession produces, is alone desired. Something analogous holds in the case of a believer in after
life, who imagines a state of personal blessedness, and
in all similar cases.

6. *Egoism Is Not the Will to Pleasure*

Thus we have determined that we cannot discover
any conduct whose motivating idea is the idea of a
state of the agent himself; and since this characteristic
is found in *no* actions, it cannot be present in the case
of "egoistic" actions. If our investigation had not led
to this negative result we should now have to inquire
whether egoistic behavior is classified with that in

which the motive is the idea of a *pleasant* personal state. But we may now ignore this question; neither a pleasant nor unpleasant state of the self is ever actually imagined.

This attempt to analyze and conceive egoism as an impulse is no longer relevant. A similar attempt, undertaken by many philosophers, which proceeds from the formula that those acts are egoistic which are directed upon personal *pleasure* as the final goal, fares even worse.

Having determined, in the previous chapter, what role pleasure really plays in volition, we recognize at once the mistake of this formulation; however, we are now in position to form a final judgment regarding it by means of the considerations just presented. While, according to the view criticized, a volition is called egoistic when the idea of a pleasant personal state functions as motive, according to the new formula the motive must be an *idea of pleasure* itself. This idea of pleasure must itself be pleasant, and egoism would thus be the impulse which is directed toward *pleasure*.

Do we really mean this by the word "egoism"? Indeed, is there any such thing? Is such a thing conceivable? If it is probable that in general no given personal state is in itself imaginable, this certainly also holds of pleasure. For pleasure and pain as emotional tones are most intimately connected with the self, with the states of the self. Psychologists usually define the feelings as contents of the consciousness of "states," in opposition, for example, to perceptions as the contents

of the consciousness of "objects." And they are almost
all agreed that there is no such thing as the "idea of a
feeling." Thus I can only *feel* pleasure and pain, I
cannot think or imagine them. It is impossible to
realize the pleasure that one has, for instance, in the
sight of a beloved face, except by imagining this face
itself; then one feels pleasure (generally less than in
the presence of the corresponding perception); a feeling is itself present, it is lived through, actually had,
not merely imagined. Moreover, one cannot imagine
an idea, but can only have it. It appears to me to be
certain that in the strict sense pleasure and pain are
unimaginable; in order to intuit them one must each
time provide them in the original. Similarly, of wrath,
fury, love, and other affections, there are really no ideas
possible. The experiences of accompanying phenomena must serve as substitutes: the outer manner of
reaction, the characteristic sensations of strain, and so
forth; in short, all that which is *perceptual,* and connected with the affection. For every idea presupposes
some perception as its pattern.

If there is no idea of pleasure, then it cannot appear
as a motive; in other words, there is no impulse toward
pleasure, and hence egoism cannot be such. Pleasure
is never desired, but only that which is imagined with
pleasure. Therefore, it is impossible to assert that egoism is the impulse directed toward one's personal welfare and that "personal welfare" can be identified with
pleasure.

7. *Egoism and the Impulse of Self-Preservation*

We need mention only one other attempt to treat selfishness as an impulse. It is its identification with the so-called "impulse of self-preservation," an idea that one may find, for example, in Spinoza. First, concerning this, we should note that the language of everyday use does not justify the equivalence; for we try to distinguish clearly between egoism and the effort of self-preservation. To begin with, not every act of self-preservation is considered "egoistic," for example, the normal care of one's health, the avoidance of unnecessary danger, defense of one's life against robbers; and, in the second place, not all "egoistic" conduct is directed toward self-preservation. The egoist thinks much more of enjoyment than of life, and can, through inconsiderate pursuit of the former, very well put the latter in jeopardy; indeed, one can think of suicide proceeding from egoism, for example, in the cases in which a life, whose preservation is of the greatest importance for others, is wilfully ended because of ennui.

These facts make it impossible to conceive egoism as an impulse of self-preservation. But even if a close connection existed between the two notions, egoism would not thereby become an "impulse"; for one cannot speak of an effort of self-preservation as an impulse in our sense. This would only be possible if there were an intuitive idea of "self-preservation," which because of its pleasure tone would incite certain kinds of conduct. But obviously "self-preservation" is such an abstract concept that there is certainly no intuitive emotional idea of it. Actually, the modes of behavior which are considered typical expressions of the effort of self-preservation are to be considered manifestations rather of a fear of death or destruction, and this too is not a simple impulse (because "destruction" also is a much too general concept), but a collective name for a class of dispositions to react with powerful unpleasant feelings in certain dangerous situations.

8. *Egoism as Inconsiderateness*

Inevitably, then, we arrive at the conclusion that egoism is not an impulse, and that to this word corresponds a complicated meaning. This meaning is of great importance for ethics, and we must inquire into it further.

Following the preceding considerations, we need no longer pursue the possibility that "egoism," although not a single impulse, might mean a common property of a series of different impulses. For these considerations showed us that the mere striving for something, the fact that some idea awakens feelings of pleasure is not itself enough to constitute "selfishness." We cannot, for example, separate out a group of "sensual impulses" and call these egoistic. (This has often been tried, apparently in the hope of finding in sense-pleasure the readiest substitute for the difficult concept of "personal welfare.") In this connection one always thinks of hunger, thirst, and the sexual impulse. And in fact one cannot extend the concept of sensual desire much further without obtaining wholly indeterminate boundaries, since the senses play an important role in the other impulses, too, as in the aesthetic ones; and the distinction between "interested" and "disinterested" pleasure, as Kant wished to formulate it is, I think, incapable of being completely carried out. Every man has these so-called sensual inclinations, and could not exist without them; but they do not make an egoist of him, not even in the moments when they determine his action. In eating, drinking and procreating a man is far from conducting himself egoistically.

Something altogether different is needed in addition. Selfishness is neither an impulse nor a collective name for a group of impulses. The satisfaction of an impulse is never in itself egoistic; but only the manner in which this occurs, only the circumstances in which it takes place can give rise to that fact which we wish to characterize by the disparaging word "egoism."

And thus we attain the important insight (perhaps first expressed in the ethics of Bishop Butler) that by the word "selfishness" a fairly complex fact is designated, namely, the existence of a certain relative strength between the inclinations. For when we charge someone with egoism we do not blame him for the presence of a certain impulse, as when we accuse him of envy or cruelty, but we condemn him because under the given conditions just this impulse led to action; we would

have demanded the omission of this act, or the commis-
sion of another. However, he would have been able
to act otherwise only if some other inclination had been
present to repress the original impulse and direct volition toward another goal; but such opposing inclinations were absent or too weak with respect to the first.
Which are these impulses whose absence or weakness
lead to selfish conduct? They are obviously the "social impulses." These are the impulses whose essence
consists in the fact that the perception or imagination
of modes of behavior or states of *fellow men* leads
directly to feelings of pleasure or pain. One may
well describe them as the *altruistic* impulses, but this
will entail an asymmetry in the use of the words "egoism" and "altruism." A man in whom the altruistic
inclinations are absent has no immediate interest in
the weal and woe of other creatures; their joys and
sorrows, even their existence, are indifferent to him so
long as he is not required indirectly (that is, by the excitement of his other impulses) to take them into consideration. And this is in fact the peculiar characteristic of the egoist—*inconsiderateness*. It is not the fact
that he follows his special impulses that makes him
hateful and blamable, but that he does so quite untroubled by the desires and needs of others. When he
pursues his ends with such inconsiderateness that he
coldly ignores the joys and sorrows of his neighbors (in
so far as he sees no connection with his own aims), when
he remains deaf and blind and cold to the happiness
and misfortune of his neighbor, then we consider him

to be an egoist, and frequently so even when otherwise we do not in the least condemn his aims.

Thus, in principle, we discover the nature of that tendency which we call by the reproachful name of selfishness; it is constituted by inconsiderateness, which is based upon the fact that among the existing inclinations the altruistic ones are relatively underdeveloped. It would, obviously, be vain labor to try to determine separately and exactly the relationship of impulses that must hold in order to designate a man as egoistic, or to ascribe to him a definite degree of this quality. Here we cannot distinguish strictly or discriminate exactly, not to speak of measuring, for we have to do throughout with vague concepts. In ethical statements we never get beyond relative, vague, qualitative comparisons. It is necessary to keep this in mind so that we may not hunt for an apparent exactness at the wrong place, which can lead to nothing but delusion.

9. *Moral Condemnation of Egoism*

Why have we troubled so much with determining the meaning of the concept of egoism? Because we have here a suitable starting point from which we can ascertain the true meaning of moral predicates in general.

Egoistic volition is for us the example of immoral volition, volition that is condemned. To condemn an act means always to desire that it should not occur. And the desire that something should not happen means (according to our earlier explanation of desire) that the idea of its happening is unpleasant. Thus, when we ask, "Why do I condemn egoistic behavior?" the question is identical in meaning with, "Why does the idea of such behavior cause me pain?" To find an answer to this is very easy. It is, "Because the selfishness of another actually causes me pain directly." For its essence is just inconsiderateness with respect to the interests of fellow men, the pursuit of personal ends at the cost of those of others. But since I belong among these others, I am in danger of suffering a restriction of my joys and an increase of my sorrows at the hands of the egoist, at least in so far as his conduct enters into my sphere of life. Where this is not the case it affects at least the feelings and lives of our fellow men, and I share in these by virtue of my social impulses; because of them I feel as my own pain the damage done to others by the egoist. His conduct means in every instance, either directly or indirectly, the increase of my feelings of pain; no wonder, then, that the idea of his behavior possesses that emotional tone which expresses itself in condemnation and censure. Each member of human society will, on an average, react to egoism with the same feelings for the same reasons. The blame and condemnation with which they oppose it *is* nothing but *moral* censure, *moral* condemnation. Thus the moral valuation made of selfishness appears to be the natural emotional reaction of society to the influence it is exposed to by egoistic persons.

In any case this is the simplest explanation, and if it

accounts for all relevant facts we shall not only have to retain it, but also we shall have to try to extend this same explanation to all other moral valuations.

We have just expressed the view that the explanation of the moral appraisement of egoism can be carried through in an analogous manner for all moral valuations. If this opinion proves to be universally valid we shall be able to express the following law as a fundamental ethical insight: the moral valuations of modes of behavior and characters are nothing but the emotional reactions with which human society responds to the pleasant and sorrowful consequences that, according to the average experience, proceed from those modes of behavior and characters.

I consider this proposition to be correct. The following observations are devoted to its proof.

CHAPTER IV

What Is the Meaning of "Moral?"

1. *The Morality of Demand and the Morality of Desire*

The single example of a moral value-judgment which has thus far concerned us was the moral condemnation of egoism. We have taken this concept in the sense in which it implies moral disapprobation, and have determined its meaning more exactly. Our discussion was begun at this point purposely, because for our currently prevailing morality the criticism of selfishness is typical.

It is characteristic of this morality that all of its most important demands end in the repression of personal desires in favor of the desires of fellow men. These demands require *considerateness,* reject egoism, and appear to range themselves against the self, in favor of the other person. (According to Fichte all immorality has its basis in "selfishness.") Our morality is essentially a morality of *renunciation.* Among religions it is Christianity and Buddhism in particular whose moral precepts are of this character. In the Mosaic decalogue, likewise, curbing of the self is the chief postulate, and this finds its external expression in the negative form of most of the commandments: "Thou shalt not—," "thou shalt not—." The positive commandments (the third and fourth) demand consideration for the desires of God and parents. It is a morality of obedience. In Christianity the emphasis is on positive altruistic behavior, as opposed to selfishness: "Thou shalt love thy neighbor."

The constant theme of this morality is consideration of others; in its precepts, too, our fellow men and society speak and express their desires and needs; they tell us how it is desired that we should act. Hence the *demand* character of this system, which Kant held to be the essence of morality. The morality of ancient classical times, the Socratic, Stoic, and Epicurean, is quite different. Its fundamental question is not, "What is demanded of me?" but, "How must I live to be happy?" It has its source in the desires of the individual, of the agent himself, and thus bears the character not of demand but of *desire*. We could ascribe autonomy to it, in opposition to the heteronomy of the morality of demand, if another meaning did not usually lay claim to this expression. The ancient classical ethics is not an ethics of self-limitation, but of self-realization, not of renunciation, but of affirmation. The subjugation of selfishness is so little characteristic of it that, subsequently, objections were often made against its egoistic tendencies. But these objections are unjust, for condemnation of egoism and consideration for others and society (for example, the state) are present in it with all desirable distinctness, although usually not in the form of an original, ultimate obligation, but as a derivative demand.

In general it should be noted that judgments of particular acts in different moral systems deviate very little from each other. Base acts (at least within one's own society) are everywhere detested, and magnanimity everywhere praised; only the spirit or state of mind from which the valuation proceeds seems different, that is, the valuation appears to be justified differently.

The search which we begin here for the meaning of the word "moral" would constitute, according to the considerations of Chapter I, a general preparatory task of ethics; and the systematic arrangements of all the cases of its use, in different times among different people, circles, and circumstances, would lead to a system of norms (or to several) upon which the causal explanation of ethics would have to base itself. But we renounce from the outset any attempt to develop such a system; we have passed at once to its peak, where the most general formulation of the concept of "moral good" is to be found. We do this because we desire to deal with the most general ethical problems, and not to concern ourselves with special moral valuations. This shortened procedure is possible because the transition from the lower to the higher levels of the system is, in practice, always necessary and constantly made; so that we may presuppose the greater part of the task to be done, even though the results do not lie before us carefully formulated. Thus we see how little the theory of norms, to which this formulation belongs, contributes to actual ethical knowledge.

An essential difference between the morality of demand and the morality of desire, between the ethics of self-limitation and that of self-assertion, is not hard to find: at bottom there lies a different concept of the *good*. With Socrates the word "good" appears to have a unified meaning; in the Platonic dialogues there is talk of good shoes, a good cobbler, a good citizen, and so forth, without any difference in meaning being apparent. In Chapter I we considered the fact that the word "good" is also used in an extra-moral sense, and suggested that moral good is a species of the universal genus "good," being distinguished from this latter by certain specific differences, but having the most important properties in common with it. Socrates and most of the ancients never doubted this, and considered the common element so exclusively that they failed altogether to inquire into the specific properties of the "moral" good. Aristotle did so and determined the specific difference very nicely when he said, When we call anyone a good cobbler or a good pilot or a good architect, we use the word in an extra-moral sense; but when we call him a good *man,* then we use the word with its moral meaning.

However, the Aristotelian formulation is no more than a hint for us, which we improve and perfect by proposing the following, in order to express the actual meaning of the word:

The word "good" has a moral sense when (1) it

refers to human *decisions,* and (2) expresses an approbation by human *society*.

In order to explain the words "approve" and "society"
we add that when we say: the decision of an individual
is "approved by society," this means: is *desired* by a
large majority of those persons with whom the individual comes into contact through word or deed. It
is essential to these statements that they be vague.

For the Greeks, originally, "good" meant nothing
but what is desired, that is, in our language, what is
imagined with pleasure (ἡδονή); therefore ancient
ethics is for the most part a theory of pleasure, hedonism. Even today "good" means, in the most general
sense, the same thing: a thing is good if it is as one desires it. But from this, under the influence of our
morality of renunciation, the narrower meaning of the
morally good has arisen. Good in *this* sense means
merely what is desired by human society, something
which confronts the individual as an *alien* desire, which
may or may not coincide with personal desires. The
desires of others are the *demands* which they make of
individuals. Hence an ethics which concerns the good
in this sense alone is not a theory of pleasure, but of
what is obligatory; it is "deontology."

The *ethical theory* of the Greeks was based on desires and not upon demands, for the Greek could not
imagine otherwise than that the individual himself
must be his own moral lawgiver; moral norms were
of course, then, as in every community, also formulated
as *commands*. Because of the fact that modern ethics

makes central the facts of demand and renunciation, it runs the risk of putting senseless questions and going wholly astray; on the other hand, its path leads nearer to certain fundamental insights of great importance for the understanding of ethical matters. For, in fact, in the concept of renunciation or in the emphasis upon altruism lies a hint leading toward the most essential point of morality.

2. *Moral Demands as Expressions of the Desires of Society*

For us it is clear that there must be no insuperable opposition between an ethics as theory of pleasure and as theory of moral obligation; or, as we may put it, between the theory of goods or pleasures and the theory of duty; but the latter will be grounded by and deduced from the former. For, according to our conception, the moral demands or duties go back in the last analysis to the feelings of pleasure and pain of individuals, since they are nothing but the average, prevailing desires of society. It is, of course, comprehensible that in practice the morality of self-realization should arrive also at demands of renunciation, which appear to be necessary means to the end of happiness. Thus the ideals of the wise man and the saint approach one another; performance of duty appears as the condition of self-realization.

If, on the other hand, the precepts of renunciation were something final and absolute, as their exponents would have us believe, and not derivable from any desires, there would be no bridge between happiness and virtue, there would be enmity or complete indifference. If a virtuous person should ever be happy this would be the merest accident, and if he were *always* happy this would be an incomprehensible miracle. A connection between the performance of duty and happiness exists, a reconciliation of the ethics of renunciation with the ethics of joy is possible, the agreement of their valuations in individual practical cases is explicable, only if moral commands themselves rise out of human needs and desires. We affirmed that this is actually the case (p. 78) when we formulated the hypothesis that the moral precepts are nothing but the expressions of the desires of human society; in the moral valuation of definite acts or dispositions as good or bad is mirrored only the measure of joy or sorrow that society expects to receive from those acts or dispositions. Thus we see how very important is the validity of the proposition made at the end of the preceding chapter; let us now devote ourselves to its proof.

In the thesis with whose proof we are concerned there are, strictly, two different assertions to be distinguished: first, that, in fact, whatever is morally approved does promise to increase the joys of human society; and second, that this effect expected by society is really the only reason *why* it is approved. It is clear that these assertions are to be distinguished carefully. It could be that everything called "morally good" by society did in fact serve to benefit society, and vice versa, but that the reason for calling it good and approving it lay elsewhere. The case (of which we convinced ourselves in the discussion of egoism) is as follows: the determination of the complete extensional equality of the concepts "morally good" and "what advances the pleasure of society" leads any unbiased person to believe also in their intensional equality; and special opposing reasons would be necessary to make this belief appear to be unjustified. Without such opposing reasons the inference to the identity of both concepts is simply obvious in terms of the method of empirical knowledge. If, in addition, we should succeed in deducing from psychological laws that behavior which is favorable to the genesis of pleasure in the human community must be approved by it, while what increases sorrow necessarily is subjected to its disapproval (as we have seen in the case of egoism), then no one will be able to upset our conviction that this approbation and disapprobation is nothing but "moral" approbation and disapprobation.

Accordingly, the proof of our thesis would involve two steps: (1) to show that in fact the moral predicate "good" is bestowed only upon such behavior as promises the social group an increase in pleasure, and (2) to refute the reasons which lead many philosophers to believe that, despite the foregoing fact, the predicate "good" *means* something different from promising an increase of happiness or a decrease of sorrow for society. For if these reasons do not hold good the validity of the second assertion is self-evident.

3. *Critique of Utilitarianism*

The first thesis which we have to defend and which asserts that "good" is what tends to further the happiness of society bears a special name in ethics; it is the moral principle of "Utilitarianism." It has this name because it says, roughly, "Good is what is useful (utile) to human society." The formulation of our thesis is perhaps not unessentially different from that which it received in the classical systems of Utilitarianism. These systems say (at least according to their sense): "The good *is* what *brings* the greatest possible happiness to society." We express it more carefully: "In human society, that is *called* good which is *believed* to bring the greatest happiness."

Is it necessary to point out the difference between these formulae? In the first it might seem (and this was actually the opinion of certain champions of the utilitarian principle) that it contains the absolute demand that everyone must set as the final goal of his action the happiness of the greatest number; while the second merely wishes to express, as a fact, the demands which society actually makes of its members.

Whoever advocates a demand must make its content as precise as possible. Hence the Utilitarian who seeks a moral principle cannot be satisfied with the vague statement that good is what furthers the "happiness of human society," but must seek to make this latter concept more exact. The inevitable attempt to attain a more exact determination led Bentham to the famous Utilitarian formula that those acts are morally good which under given circumstances have the "greatest happiness of the greatest number of human beings" (or living creatures in general?) as their consequences. A few words can show the utter inapplicability of this formula.   In the first place, the results of every act are simply incalculable, for they stretch on into time indefinitely; and even the resultant events of the near future cannot be predicted, for they depend more or less upon "chance," that is, slightly differing acts can have extraordinarily different effects.   In the second place, "the greatest happiness of the greatest number" is a senseless conjunction of words, which can indeed be given a meaning by means of certain conventions, but such a conventional meaning, because of its arbitrariness, will not express the thought which the formula would like to express.   Furthermore, Utilitarianism did not attempt to find a meaningful convention, but believed that these words had a clear meaning, presupposing that one can speak of the pleasure of different persons as of something comparable in magnitude. And this is the fundamental mistake.   If it has been shown (p. 40) that even the individual feelings of pleasure are not amenable to quantitative comparison, then this holds even more of the vague concept of happiness, which is difficult to construct in any way except as a sort of conjunction or "summation" of feelings of pleasure.   The Utilitarian would find himself confronted by such questions as these: "How should I act when the circumstances are such that my conduct can lead either to a certain definite amount of happiness in each of four persons, or double that amount for each of two?" The absurdity of such a question is apparent; but the Utilitarian cannot avoid them; his formula makes sense only if he can tell us exactly what it means to say, "*A* is three-and-a-half times as happy as *B*."

We are in a better situation with respect to this matter than are the followers of Bentham; for we do not wish, as they do, to establish a formula or a command. We do not desire to construct a concept of the "good" —which we should have to define exactly—but we want only a simple determination of what, in human society, is held to be good. Thus we are not required to state of what the highest good consists, and which modes of behavior lead to it; we determine only that men *believe,* on the average, and are in wide agreement, that certain modes of behavior lead to the greatest common good. The reasons for this belief do not at present interest us, and whether they are *good* reasons, whether they are *valid,* we are not required to know by our formulation of the question.

One other important observation is here included: every philosopher, including the Utilitarian, knows of course that no one can predict the results of conduct with complete assurance, that this is always in part an effect of chance. If, despite this, Utilitarianism or any other ethical theory apparently judges the moral value of a decision by its results, this can only be the average or *probable* result. It has always been evident that the *decisions* (the "intentions") alone are the objects of moral judgment. Therefore it is incorrect to distinguish, as is often done, between an "ethics of intention" and an "ethics of result." There has never been an "ethics of result."

4. *The Good Appears to Society as the Useful*

In order to show that that is considered "morally good" which, *according to the opinion of society,* is to its advantage (pleasure increasing) we must establish that moral valuations of modes of behavior change when the structure of human society changes, and that this change takes place in a manner which is inevitable if the opinion entertained regarding the conditions of the welfare of society is determinative of that valuation. For if it appears that the actual alteration of moral valuations corresponds to changes of certain states of, and opinions in, the community, then we may with certainty assume that these states and views represent the basis upon which the valuations rest.

This is actually the case. Ethnography and history agree in teaching that the diversities in moral precepts, which change from people to people and epoch to epoch, always correspond to diversities in what, under the prevailing circumstances, is favorable to the welfare of the society; or rather to what is so considered. We here point to a single set of facts in which this alteration shows itself especially clearly, namely, the change in moral views correlated with the increase in *size* of the community in which they prevail. In such times and places in which the community of persons (determined by their instinctive drawing together in the common struggle for existence) extends over only a small tribe, a clan, or a family, the moral rules that are recognized demand consideration only for the members of the group itself; with respect to those who stand outside it there is no ethical obligation. Often, indeed, everyone who does not belong to the group is *eo ipso* considered an enemy, an outlaw. It is well known that in primitive tribes under certain circumstances the murder of a member of a neighboring tribe is considered to be as great a moral service as the murder of a member of one's own tribe would be a crime.

And these valuations are not merely proclaimed externally and recognized by the individual because of the application of sanctions, but appear to him as the voice of his own conscience, which commands him with incontrovertible authority and terrible emotional force (for, obviously, the conscience is formed by external suggestion, whose whisperings resound in the mind as through a powerful trumpet). We find a famous example of this in the writings of Darwin, who tells of the dreadful pangs of conscience suffered by an African savage who had neglected to take revenge on a neighboring tribe for injury done him by some sort of magic. A missionary had impressed upon him that it is a great sin to murder a man, and the savage did not dare to carry out the act of vengeance. But the consciousness of his neglected "duty" oppressed him so much that he went about disturbed and upset, rejected food and drink, and could enjoy nothing. In short, he showed all the signs of an "evil conscience." Finally he could bear it no longer, stole away secretly, slew a member of the other clan and returned light of heart: he had performed his duty and pacified his conscience by means of the murder. Would anyone wish to deny that the feelings of the savage are "real" pangs of conscience, as these are felt by a moral civilized man? If so, we can only attribute this to prejudice, for one will search in vain for the difference. Of course, in general, the European feels scruples of conscience under different circumstances, namely, after committing murder, and not when the deed has been omitted; but even this does not hold without exceptions. For in *war* the great majority of men consider the destruction of their enemies to be not only not forbidden, but actually a moral obligation.

The difference between the moral views of the African and a modern European in this respect is explained by the fact that the group which furnishes the standard for the formation of those views is for the savage the tribe or clan, but for the civilized man is extended to include a whole nation or state; and further upon the fact that the state of enmity is enduring for the one, and transitory for the other. And if to a philosopher war between two nations appears quite as immoral as a conflict between two armed bands of a single nation, this is because for him the human society which makes the moral laws has extended over the whole world: in his conscience re-echoes the voice of all humanity.

What appears here in a single example holds universally. The content of the moral precepts that hold in a community, and that are taken over completely into the moral consciousness of its members, depends entirely upon its living conditions, upon its size and strength, its relation to the surrounding world, its civilization, customs, and religious ideas. I forego the introduction of further evidence, and refer to Westermarck's *Origin and Development of Moral Ideas,* and to Spencer's *Data of Ethics,* which contain rich material. We see in the dependence of moral valuations upon the states of human society a sure indication that the content of morality is actually determined by society. It also seems to be the moral lawgiver concerning whom (according to Chapter I) ethics must inquire. We shall soon see whether this result is final or requires a more thorough proof.

5. *The Formulation of Moral Laws Takes Place According to the Utilitarian Principle*

Closer examination of the content of moral precepts shows that the community anticipates a furtherance of its welfare from their observance. It is not necessary to prove this in particular cases, since it is generally not disputed. For whatever be one's opinion regarding the nature and origin of moral rules, it is generally believed that society is benefited if all of its members obey them.[1]   For the confirmation of this we point out that everywhere the laws promulgated by the state (which are not, indeed, identical with moral laws, but which still should represent their essential minimum) are thought out with no other purpose in mind than to advance the general welfare.   It is inconceivable that any modern lawmaker could give any other justification for the proposal of a law than this utilitarian one (the lawmaker always appears as a utilitarian because he says in justification of his proposals, "They *are* useful to society," not, "Society considers them to be useful").   Whenever legislatures or parliaments discuss a law or precept the discussion centers solely on the question, "Which decision will be *most* useful to society?"   No one asks, "Which decision is moral or has the greatest moral value?"   It may happen that in debate mention is made of the "honor" of the community or the "holiness" of an institution is stressed, but such arguments are never directed *against* the increase of happiness, but are introduced only when it is silently assumed that the observance of them does not stand in opposition to society's striving for happiness.   The lawmakers have thus the unenviable task of deciding what *in fact* will be most advantageous to the welfare of the state or humanity.   And they do not despair of the solution of this task only because they can, generally,

---

[1] An exception is found in Mandeville's famous *The Fable of the Bees* or *Private Vices Public Benefits*.

replace it by an easier one, namely: to hinder what would directly injure society. In so doing they make the (not self-evident) assumption that the avoidance of immediate injury is likewise the path to the greatest general welfare.

What holds of the formulated laws, of legality, also holds for the moral views of society, for the moral code: the conviction prevails that moral behavior furthers the general happiness, indeed that it is the necessary if not the sufficient condition of that happiness. The opposing view has been held occasionally by a few individuals, but that need not surprise us, for there is hardly any possible opinion regarding matters of human importance which has not been expressed by someone. If many philosophers proclaim with great feeling that morality is independent of welfare, by saying that one must always do what is "right," even though one sees clearly that the greatest harm will result, then such a standpoint of "*fiat justitia, pereat mundus*" does indeed partake of the sublime, which is always the attribute of the unconditioned; but no wise guide of a nation's destiny would actually assume the responsibility of acting according to that prescription. And to the blame he would thus receive from the absolutist philosopher would be opposed the praise that a grateful society would bestow upon him for not having sacrificed its well-being in favor of an abstract principle. Society would unquestionably consider his behavior to be morally good. Of course the divergent attitude of the philosopher must also be made intelligible; we must

understand how he arrives at his approbations and dis-
approbations. We shall deal with this question in a
moment.

6. *Conclusions*

By means of considerations like the foregoing we arrive at the following results:

(1) The meaning of the word "good" (that is,
what is considered as moral) is determined by the opinion of society, which is the lawgiver formulating moral
demands. Since, with respect to a social group, there
can only be an *average* or prevailing opinion, one cannot raise an objection to this view based upon the fact
that there are deviations from some of the usual norms.

(2) The content of the concept "good" is determined in such a way by society that all and only those
modes of behavior are subsumed under it which society believes are advantageous to its welfare and preservation (which is indeed the presupposition of its welfare).

Considering propositions (1) and (2) together we
deduce from them, or consider the assertion justified,
that:

(3) The moral demands are established by society
only because the fulfillment of these demands appears
to be useful to it.

We can also formulate proposition (3) by saying,
"The good is good only because it is considered by society to be useful"; and in the last analysis this means:

considered to be conducive to pleasure. Or also thus: the *material* meaning of the word "moral" *exhausts itself* in denoting what, according to the prevailing opinion in society, is advantageous (its *formal* meaning consists in being demanded by society).

It is clear that a logical connection must exist between (1) and (2); for the reason that moral behavior is demanded must somehow or other lie in the nature of morality, and if this nature is completely given by proposition (2) it must contain the grounds of (1). But this connection need not be as direct and simple as proposition (3) would make out. It might be that even though morality were undoubtedly advantageous to the general welfare it would be approved upon *other* grounds. In other words, it might be that the idea of moral behavior did not owe its pleasure-tone to belief in the usefulness of such behavior to society, but that this joy had some other origin, for example, in a "conscience," whose presence expressed itself in certain special feelings and ideas (or actually was composed of them) and whose origin constituted a special problem. We mention for example the metaphysical hypothesis that divine insight furnished man with a conscience in order to implant in him a motive of moral behavior, such behavior as would be (again according to the divine insight) in the last analysis most useful to him. We require no such hypotheses, however, for what they would explain is explained for us by known psychological relationships. As soon, that is, as one feels himself to be a member of society and feels his own good and evil to be bound up with that of others, the idea of a happy community must become a pleasant idea; and this emotional tone extends itself according to known laws to all modes of behavior which he supposes are advantageous to the welfare of society. In other words: a social man *desires* that his environment be happy and unendangered, desires all modes of behavior which are conducive to this, values, approves and commends them, and condemns and persecutes contrary conduct. All these are only different ways of saying the same thing.

Of course the processes whereby the general welfare becomes a pleasant goal are complicated; and one must not, above all, attribute too great a role to rational *insight*. For even if men thought much more and more accurately than they usually do about the consequences of action, such considerations would have but little influence in the realm of feelings. And these processes take place chiefly in this realm, in the absence of subtle thinking. But here we can appeal to a general principle which has otherwise proved to be valid in psychology and biology, namely, that the result of organic, unconscious, or instinctive processes is the same as would have resulted from a rational calculation. This principle is closely connected with that general "purposiveness" of the organic world which is usually called "teleology." If one would trace the development of these psychic processes, one must keep specially in mind that they have their origin in concrete situations, and that such abstract concepts as the "general welfare" are quite useless in the formation of powerful centers of feeling. In what follows we shall have occasion to offer contributions to the psychology of moral valuation, but at present we are satisfied to see at least the path along which the human spirit necessarily arrives at the praise and approbation of "moral" behavior.

With this we have not of course strictly shown that the valuation of morality, which we have deduced, is actually *moral valuation* (that it does not merely constitute the basis of a certain type of value of the moral life, a "utility value," but constitutes the whole of moral valuation); but we shall, according to our program, consider it certain and thus hold our proposition (3) (p. 97) to be true if we also succeed in showing that the most important attempt in ethics to conceive the nature of moral valuation differently cannot be carried out. Our only reasons for considering this attempt at all are historical; apart from them, considered factually, what has been adduced appears to us to contain a sufficient foundation of our thesis, however inexhaustive it may be. But since, especially at present, many philosophical writers represent a very different point of view, we turn to the *critical* considerations, which we proposed as the second stage in the proof of our thesis (p. 86).

CHAPTER V

Are There Absolute Values?

1. *The Theory of Objective Values*

The opinion we have to examine may best be expressed negatively in the assertion that the moral value of a disposition cannot in any way be grounded in feelings of pleasure. Value is something wholly independent of our feelings, something pertaining to valuable objects, in a definite amount and degree, quite independently of the way in which we react emotionally to them, and to whether anyone acknowledges the value or not. Pleasure, to be sure, is a value, but only one among many, and obviously not the highest. Often it is admitted that the valuable produces feelings of pleasure in the observer, but this fact is supposed to have nothing to do with the *essence* of the value, but is, in a sense, accidental. I say "in a sense," for many who hold this view do not wish, I believe, to deny that perhaps the generation of feelings of pleasure in the presence of something valuable is a natural law, and that a causal connection exists between the two. But they say that this is quite unessential, that if it were not so it would make no difference to the value of the valuable thing; this value would exist even if the law of nature read: "The idea of the valuable thing is quite indifferent to all men," or "extremely annoying" or "horrible."

The role played in ethics by this theory of the objectivity of value is too well known to require one to dwell upon it. It proclaims the existence of a system of values, which, like the Platonic ideas, constitutes a realm independent of actuality, and in which is exhibited an essential order of such a nature that the values compose a hierarchy arranged according to higher and lower. And its relation to reality is only established by the moral command, which runs, approximately, "Act so that the events or things produced by your actions are as valuable as possible."

The criticism which we make of this view is extremely simple. Its main lines are prescribed by our philosophical method. We ask *first*, "What does the word value *mean*?" or, which comes to the same thing, "What is the meaning of an assertion which ascribes a certain value to any object?" This question can be answered only by stating the method of determining the truth of a value judgment; that is, one must state exactly under what empirical conditions the proposition "This object is valuable" is true, and under what conditions it is false. If one cannot state these conditions, then the proposition is a meaningless combination of words.

Thus we ask the philosopher, "How do you recognize the value of an object?" And since no one is here to answer (the author writes these lines in deep seclusion on the rocky coast of the Adriatic Sea) we shall search for the usual and possible answers together.

2. *Pleasure as the Criterion of Objective Value*

(*a.*) In case anyone (I do not know whether there is any such person) should answer that values are in fact to be recognized only in feelings of pleasure which valuable things awaken in us, and that also the rank of the value is disclosed to us only by means of the intensity of the corresponding feeling, and that in addition there is no other criterion of the existence and rank of the value, yet that nevertheless the value does not *consist* in the activity of producing pleasure, but is something else, then we must accuse him of logical nonsense. However, we do it very unwillingly, for factually we do not find anything to dispute regarding the consequences of his theory. The nonsense consists in the fact that with respect to all *verifiable* consequences his view is in complete agreement with our own (that "value" is nothing but a name for the dormant pleasure possibilities of the valuable object), but despite this he asserts that they are different. The proposition that "to be valuable" means something quite different from "to bring pleasure" presupposes that there is some property which belongs only to the valuable, and not to the pleasure-bringing: the assertion becomes senseless if pleasure-producing is the *only* characteristic of the valuable. If we should peacefully grant the existence of "objective" value, this would be nothing but a content-less addition. Everything would remain as if it were essentially subjective, for we would be able to make an assertion about it only because of its pleasure consequences, as is also the case according to our own view. I add that from the criticized standpoint every feeling of pleasure must be interpreted as the sign of an objective value. If this held only in certain cases, but not in others, we should have to be able to say how the cases differed, and this would require a new criterion and the rejection of the original one, which was simply pleasure. The advocate of objective values requires, then, an empirical criterion of value which cannot be identical with pleasure.

3. Objective Criteria of Value?

(b.) It is natural to want to give an objective criterion for objective values—just as we recognize that an animal is a camel by the fact that it has two humps, concerning whose existence one can convince himself by sense-perception. Sense-perception, whose value as a criterion for objectivity has often been disputed in epistemological considerations, may be unhesitatingly accepted as the judge in our problem, as in all questions of daily life. Hence if value could be seen or touched as can a camel's hump, ethics would have no occasion to discuss its nature. But since this is not so, one seeks some objective fact which shall serve as the sign of values; and thus one asserts, for example,

"Whatever furthers the progress of evolution is valuable," or, "Whatever contributes to the creation of spiritual possessions, for example, works of art, and science, is valuable," or similar statements. If I am not mistaken, Wilhelm Wundt in his ethics of objective spiritual products made such an attempt.

We feel at once what is wrong in such attempts. Even if one should succeed in finding a formula which fitted everything generally considered to be valuable, such a formula, it seems to me, would always appear to be circular. Since, for example, what a "spiritual possession" is, what shall pass for an "upward evolution" (as opposed to downward) can only be determined by comparison with some standard. It cannot itself determine the standard. And if, in order to escape the circle, one arbitrarily establishes what should be understood by spiritual possessions, and things of the sort, this determination would be arbitrary; at best one would have produced the definition of a concept, based upon opinion, which one decides to call "value"; but this would not offer a criterion for *that* which we all *mean* when we use the word "value."

A fundamental error lies at the basis of the whole attempt: it consists in seeking value distinctions in the objective facts themselves, without reference to the acts of preference and selection, through which alone value comes into the world.

4. *Subjective Criteria of Value*

(*c.*) Thus there remains no alternative to locating the characteristic of value once more in an immediate datum and to finding the verification of a proposition concerning value in the occurrence of a definite experience. Our own criterion is of this sort: the corresponding experience is simply the feeling of pleasure, with which we dealt at length in Chapter II. According to our opinion the *essence* of value is completely exhausted by it. The opposing theory of absolute value cannot, as was shown in (*a.*), use pleasure as the characteristic of value; it must therefore assert the occurrence of a wholly different experience which indicates the existence of a value. This is, in fact, if I understand them rightly, the opinion of the noteworthy representatives of that theory (of Brentano, and the schools following him). According to them we possess the capacity of determining the existence of a value in much the same way as we are acquainted with the presence of a material object by means of perception. The role here played by sensation is there taken over by a specific experience, which one may call the feeling or experience of value, insight, or what not; without of course contributing anything to a closer description by this naming. In any case, it is always something ultimate, unanalyzable, which must appear when a value judgment is verified, and which one either has or does not have, concerning which therefore there can be no further discussion.

What should we say regarding this theory? In so far as it asserts the existence of a special datum of consciousness, a "value-experience," any disagreement would be senseless, for each person alone can know what he experiences. One could simply accept or reject the theory without any proof. (I personally could not accept it, because I do not succeed in distinguishing between the feeling of pleasure that I have when I hear "Don Juan" or see a noble face or read about the personality of Abraham Lincoln, and an elementary value-experience which, according to that view, must first assure me that what gives me joy is also a *value*.)

But the theory asserts not only the existence or occurrence of a certain datum of consciousness, but asserts further that this informs me of something objective, independent of me, that it guarantees for me the existence of an absolute value. Does this assertion also not require verification? That the criterion is finally found in a datum of consciousness, that is, in the realm of the "subjective," would not in itself be suspicious; for this cannot be avoided, and the example of perception teaches us that "subjective" sensations can lead us to objects whose independence of us, and objectivity, leave for all practical purposes nothing to be desired. And in ethics we are concerned with practical knowledge in the significant sense. But the sensations are able to carry out that performance only because they obey very definite *laws*. The play of perceptions, however colorful it be, exhibits a very definite regularity, which is expressed by the fact that we are able to make verifiable predictions concerning the occurrence of sensations. (Regularity does not indicate something objective, but is itself objectivity.) If something of the sort held of the hypothetical value-feelings, as holds for sensations; if value propositions cohered in a consistent system, as do the propositions about perceptions, *then* value-feelings could guarantee objective values. But that is not the case. The chaos of valuations is proverbial, and there is no hope of putting value theory, ethics and aesthetics, on a level with physics, which would otherwise be easy.

Thus there is no possibility of passing from elementary value-experiences to the justification of objective absolute values. But if one says that the justification lies already contained within the experience itself I can only answer that I cannot imagine how such an assertion would be verified, and that therefore I do not know what it means.

5. *Do Value Judgments Have the Validity of Logico-Mathematical Propositions?*

(*d.*) Perhaps many hold the comparison of absolute values to objective material bodies to be improper, because the realm of values seems incomparable to gross physical reality. At least we hardly ever find the analogy to perception drawn.[1] Instead of it, the more often, another, that is, the value-propositions are compared to the propositions of logic or mathematics, and explained by means of them. Neither deals with "actual" objects, and the validity of both is of the same sort. In the example of logic or mathematics we see best, it is supposed, how it is possible, despite the subjectivity of our experience of evidence, to arrive at what is intrinsically valid, absolute, and existing independently of any assent or any act of thought or feeling. The law of contradiction, and the proposition "Two times two equals four" hold simply, whether anyone thinks and understands them or not. As here with absolute truth, so there with absolute value. The notion of the objectivity of value is usually made plausible in this way (for example, see Nicolai Hartmann, *Ethics*), and generally it remains the *only* way.

But, however misleading the argument is, our comparison with perception and its objects is a thousand times better, even from the standpoint of the absolutist theory. A comparison of any propositions with those of logic (which in this context also include the mathematical) always leads to nonsense; for logic is simply not comparable to anything (I hope I may be forgiven this somewhat paradoxical statement, but the way in which even today the essence of logic is misunderstood

---

[1] Nevertheless the advocates of absolute values often say that these are *intuitively* known, and their whole outlook is thus called "intuitionism," a term in use in particular among English writers. But intuition signifies something similar to perception.

demands forthright criticism). This is not the place for me to expand this point; I note briefly only that the propositions of logic and the so-called propositions of mathematics are tautologies, or tautology-like forms, that is, they express nothing whatever (they are merely rules for the transformation of propositions). It is to this alone that they owe their absolute (independent of every experience) truth, which is really only a meaningless limiting case of truth. Thus in logic it is not as, according to the hopes or statements of the absolutists, it should be in value theory: namely, that here, in some sense, there is a realm of non-actual essences, independent of us, but ready to be recognized by us at any time, or, perhaps, in the case of values, to be realized. Logical propositions furnish us with no knowledge whatever, they express no facts, and teach us nothing about what exists in the world, or how anything does or should behave in the world. Thus if the value-propositions were similar to them it would only follow that they too were mere tautologies, in all strictness saying nothing; a consequence that would certainly cause us to wish value-propositions to have as little similarity as possible to those of logic. Judgments about value ought to tell us just what is most important.

Tautological propositions can be formed about anything, and of course, about values. When, for example, I write the proposition: "If the value A is greater than the value B, then the value B is smaller than the value A," I have clearly said in this true proposition nothing at all about values, but have merely shown the equivalence of two different modes of expression. Indeed the proposition is not a proposition of value theory, but belongs to logic. And so it is always: whenever I come upon a proposition that is true independently of every experience, I am in the realm of logic. Only the propositions of logic, and all of them, have this character. In this lies their peculiarity, which I spoke of before.

Thus also in a comparison with logic and mathematics we fail to find a verifiable meaning in propositions about absolute values.

6. *The "Absolute Ought"*

(*e.*) Here it is necessary to bestow a moment's attention upon Kant's ethics. His concept of *ought* represents exactly what we have hitherto called "value-experience." There was undoubtedly at work in him a motive which presumably also plays a role in the genesis of modern absolutist theories: the desire to elevate ethics entirely above the empirical level. Kant showed correctly that the moral precepts have the character of demands, and that each appears to us as an "ought." But he could not bring himself to leave its empirical meaning to this word, in which alone it is actually used. Everyone knows this meaning: "I ought to do something" never means anything but "Someone wants me to do it." And in fact the desire of another, directed upon me, is described as an ought only when that person is able to add pressure to his desire and thus to reward fulfillment and to punish neglect, or at least to point out the natural consequences of observance or neglect. This is the meaning the word has in daily life; nor does it occur there with any other meaning. We call such a desire a command (imperative); therefore it is of the essence of the imperative to be hypothetical, that is, to presuppose some sanction, a promise or a threat.

According to our own view, developed in the previous chapter, the lawgiver who sanctions the moral commands is human society, which is furnished with the necessary power to command. Thus we may rightly say that morality makes demands on men, that they *ought* to behave in certain ways; because we use the word "ought" here in exactly the determined empirical sense. But, as we said, Kant cannot be satisfied with this. No matter whom he might find to be the source of the ethical command it would always be hypothetical, dependent upon the power and desire of this being, ceasing upon his absence or with a change of his desires. Since Kant, in order to avoid the hypothetical, did not wish to make even God responsible for the moral rules, there remained for him nothing but a leap into the void. He explained that the ought proceeded from *no* "other"; it is an absolute ought, and the ethical command is a categorical, not a conditional, imperative.

But we have seen that a relationship to a power which expresses its desires is *essential* to the concept of the

ought, just as essential as the relationship to some conditions (sanctions) is for the concept of the imperative.
These characteristics belong to the definition of both
concepts as we know them. Thus, for example, the
concept "uncle" is defined relative to nephews and
nieces; an "absolute uncle" would be nonsense. Since
Kant, for his concepts of the ought and of the imperative, expressly repudiates the relation to one who commands, and to sanctions, both terms must have for him
a wholly different meaning from that explained by us.
It is, of course, the privilege of every author to use
words as he pleases, and to give the terms he finds in
daily life a new meaning, *if only he defines this meaning exactly* and retains it.   But Kant does not give a
new definition.   He speaks as if the word "ought" is
used by him in the usual sense, minus only its relative
character.   However, this is a *contradiction,* for relativity, the relation to another desiring person, is con-
stitutive of the ought in its usual sense.   It is just as if
Kant had said, "I wish to use the phrase 'to take a
walk' with such a meaning that I can say 'a walk is
being taken' without anyone there who takes it."   An
ought without someone who gives commands is an
uncle who is such, not relatively to some nephew or
niece, but simply in himself.

In order to rid the Kantian ethics of this nonsense
we must use the word "ought" with a meaning which
has nothing in common with its original meaning;
and therefore the same word should not be used.   The
role which it plays, apart from that unfortunate ex-

planation in Kant's ethics, is, as has been suggested, that which fell to the "value-experience" in the views considered earlier, with the here unessential difference that it exclusively represents the *moral* values: it is the "moral law in me." (By the "in me" there is apparently given to Kant another opportunity to introduce a lawgiver of the ought, namely the ego itself. However, not the empirical ego—otherwise the ought would simply be the expression of its will—but the super-empirical "practical reason" of the ego, which makes it "autonomous." And in his metaphysics Kant finally also adds the sanctions in the form of other-worldly rewards.) "The practical reason" which lays down the moral law is, however, either an empty word or it reveals itself in some verifiable experience. It could be defined only in terms of such. Accordingly, for Kant the ought is to be defined as the consciousness of moral value. But with this we arrive at the problem of section (*d.*), and we may consider the untenability of this view to be established.

Still, it may be asked, might there not perhaps be given with the word "ought" at least some hint regarding the kind of psychological properties the asserted "feeling of value" would have, so that we might know where to seek for such a subtle experience, alleged to be so different from every feeling of pleasure? Is there not, perhaps, in consciousness a demonstrable experience of the "ought" complementary to that of "volition"?

We must answer that volition itself is not an

elementary experience, but is resolvable into a series of processes (cf. Chapter II), and therefore one cannot well speak of an elementary experience opposed to it. When the command of another person confronts me under the conditions described on page 110, then definite conscious processes take place in me, which represent just that experience which in everyday life we call "ought." It is complex, yet not so difficult to analyze. The decisive thing is the consciousness of "compulsion," which consists of the fact that a persistent idea is established by the one who commands, and is equipped by means of his sanctions with feeling tones so strong that they affect adversely the pleasure components of all other ideas, and (in the case of obedience) suppress them. The ought stands in opposition to something *desired,* but not to volition; the ought is rather a part of the motivation process, and as such itself belongs to volition, and does not stand in opposition to it. We seek in vain for another immediate experience of the ought.

One more point. The ought, before it can, and in order that it may, occur must also be *willed.* Kant strove in vain to make conceivable [2] how the ought, which with him had the extremely abstract character of a moral "law," could be taken up into volition; and this difficulty seems to me to exist for every absolutist

---

[2] Kant, *Critique of Practical Reason.* "How a law can be immediately and in itself the determining ground of volition (which is the essence of all morality) is for human reason an insoluble problem."

theory. In order that the valuable be actually sought and realized it must arouse our feelings. Why then does anyone oppose the recognition of the essence of value in this excitation of feeling? For one cannot make values comprehensible here below after they have been removed into a ὑπερουράνιος τόπος.[3] The assertion that *moral* values in particular have nothing to do with pleasure and pain is certainly false, for no one can deny that a feeling of *joy* is bound up with the act of moral approbation, and that one always expresses moral blame unwillingly, with pain or anger. Otherwise there is no real disapprobation, but it is only pretended.

7. The Emptiness of the Hypothesis of Absolute Values

Thus we come to the second argument against objective values, which is quite conclusive, and which frees us from and raises us above the hair-splitting that we, perhaps, began to feel in the line of thought of the first argument. This (beginning on p. 102) simply asked for the *meaning* of so-called absolute value judgments, and concluded that none could be shown, however one tried.

But now let us assume that the desired meaning has been found, so that we are able to determine in some way that there is a hierarchy of objective values wholly independent of our feelings. We now consider "value"

---

[3] [Place above the heavens.]

to be a property of objects, qualifying them in various forms (for example, beautiful, good, sublime, and so forth) and in different degrees. All these possible properties together form a system, and in each case is unambiguously determined which of these properties a specific object has, and to what degree; thereby assigning to it a definite position in the system of the value hierarchy.

Good, we say, let it be so! What follows? What have we to do with that? *How does it concern us?*

The only interest we could take in this realm of values would be a purely scientific interest; that is, it might be of interest to an investigator that the things in the world, in addition to other properties, also have these, and by means of them can be ordered in a certain way; and he might devote much labor to the description of this system. But for life and conduct this arrangement would be no more important than, say, the arrangement of the stars in the order of their magnitudes, or the serial arrangement of objects according to the alphabetical order of their names in the Swahili language.

This is no exaggeration or misrepresentation, but is actually the case. To my question, "What do these objective values mean to me?" the absolutist answers, "They constitute the guiding lines of your conduct! In setting up your goals of action you should prefer the higher to the lower." If I then ask, "Why?" the abso-

lutist simply cannot give any answer. This is the
decisive point, that because of his thesis of the independence of values, the absolutist has cut himself off
from all possibility of giving any other answer to my
question, "What happens if I don't do it?" than "Then
you don't do it, that is all!" Should he answer, "In
that case you are not a good man," then we should
note that this answer is relevant and can influence my
action only if I desire, or have reason to desire, to be a
"good man," that is, only if it is presupposed that certain feelings are connected with that concept. And
just such a presupposition may not be made by the
absolutist; he may not say, "You will be more highly
respected as a good man, you will lead a happier life,
you will have a better conscience, you will be more at
peace with yourself," and so forth; for in doing so he
appeals to my feelings, as though the value were really
binding upon me only because it brought me joy; and
this doctrine is expressly repudiated. Even though in
every way it were pleasant to me to be a scoundrel,
and if I had the cordial respect of others, genuine peace
in my soul, and pure inner joy as a result (imagine this
in a lively manner, though it is difficult to do so, because the fact is otherwise), if, thus, my life were more
agreeable, exalted and happier because of my failure
to obey the moral laws, still the absolutist would have
to say, "Yet you must obey them, even though you become extremely unhappy." Whether happy or unhappy, pleasant or unpleasant, all this has, for the in-
tuitionist, absolutely nothing to do with moral value—

which has been emphasized by no one more sharply than by Kant. But in these philosophers we still always find a hidden appeal to the feelings, even though it consist only in the use of certain honorific terms, like "honorable" itself.

Perhaps the philosopher is even proud that he cannot answer the question, "What do absolute values mean to me? What happens if I pay no attention to them?" Perhaps he even despises our question. If so, we answer his proud silence with the statement that in all seriousness we simply have no concern with such values, to which it makes no difference whether we are concerned with them or not, whose existence has no influence upon our peace of mind, our joy or sorrow, upon all those things that interest us in life. Indeed we *cannot* be concerned with such "values," for (see Chapter II) only those objects can arouse our volition which in some way or other arouse feelings of pleasure or pain in us. They would not be values for us.

Thus we conclude: if there were values which were "absolute" in the sense that they had absolutely nothing to do with our feelings, they would constitute an independent realm which would enter into the world of our volition and action at no point; for it would be as if an impenetrable wall shut them off from us. Life would proceed as if they did not exist; and for ethics they would not exist. But if the values, in addition to and without injuring their absolute existence, also had the property or power of influencing our feelings, then they would enter into our world; but only in so far

as they thus affected us. Hence values also exist for
ethics only to the extent that they make themselves felt,
that is, are relative to us. And if a philosopher says,
"Of course, but they *also* have an absolute existence,"
then we know that these words add nothing new to
the verifiable facts, that therefore they are empty, and
their assertion meaningless.

CHAPTER VI

Are There Worthless Joys and Valuable Sorrows?

1. *The Relativity of Values*

After having answered in the negative the question of the existence of absolute values, we feel finally assured of the assertion that the sense of every proposition concerning the value of an object consists in the fact that this object, or the idea of it, produces a feeling of pleasure or pain in some feeling subject. A value exists only with respect to a subject, it is relative. If there were no pleasure and pain in the world there would be no values. Everything would be indifferent.

It is well to note in what sense relativity characterizes every value: its existence depends upon the being and the feeling of a subject, but this subjectivity is not caprice, it does not mean that the subject can at will declare the object to be valuable or valueless. So long as toothaches are painful they have *no* value for the sufferer, and he cannot alter this; otherwise he would certainly do so. When a specific object in a specific relation is presented to a specific subject, and the momentary constitution and disposition of the subject is fixed, then the feeling with which the subject reacts to the constitution of the object is also determined, that is, it has at that moment an unambiguous value or disvalue. This fact is wholly *objective;* neither the subject nor the disinterested observer can explain it away in the least; the fact is just as "objective" as would be the existence of an "absolute" value. The relativity of values does not therefore mean a metaphysical relativity, so to speak, as if value were no longer tangible or definite. This seems so clear to me that I would not waste a word on it if misunderstandings regarding this point did not occur (as in Nicolai Hartmann's *Ethics*). The pleasure or pain which the subject experiences in valuing is certainly something absolute, for if the word "absolute" is permissible anywhere, then it is certainly so in reference to such a final datum of consciousness. In order that an object be valuable to a subject, the object and the subject must be of a definite nature, and there must be a definite relation between them. If all this exists, then the object necessarily and unambiguously has a definite value for the subject.

This doctrine of the relativity of values, in my opinion, does full justice in every way to their true nature. It is so natural and obvious that even in ancient times it was widely held. I believe that one can trace the derivation of values from pleasure in the Socratic theory; it was expressly formulated in the Cyrenaic school founded by Aristippus, a follower of Socrates, and since that time has remained in the history of ethics. In addition, the theory is in such complete agreement with experience as it expresses itself in human institutions, that, had it not met with strong emotional opposition, no other view could have arisen. But propositions of the theory are of such a sort that the thoughts connected with them can easily give rise to unpleasant feelings, while the absolute value theory meets certain human needs, that is, its thoughts are received with pleasure. And since these emotional reactions occur in the course of ethical considerations the disapprobation of one theory and the approbation of the other itself easily takes on the character of a moral valuation; and there arises that situation of a peculiar confusion of insight and valuation that makes ethical discussions so difficult, and makes observations like those of the preceding chapter necessary.

2. *The Prejudice Against Pleasure*

A definite prejudice is to blame for the fact that the proposition asserting the relativity of value, and its dependence upon the pleasure of the evaluator, arouses unpleasant thoughts, and thus calls forth a disapprobation which appears as moral disapprobation itself. We meet this prejudice in this context again and again, and it may be considered the typical prejudice of moral philosophers: the prejudice against "pleasure." We have touched upon it lightly in earlier chapters, but it is well to examine it again systematically, for in so doing we shall be able to clarify certain more fundamental problems.

Hence we seek the psychological cause of this prejudice; and, according to the principle that an error is
first overcome when it is not only refuted but when
also its origin is explained, we shall only be safe from
the main errors of ethics when we have found that
cause.

Our question is: Why does one rebel against the
recognition of pleasure as the final measure of all value,
including moral value? It will be answered when we
explain psychologically why the word "pleasure"—or
words having similar meaning—has the tendency to be
unpleasant. We must, conversely, also seek the reason
why suffering and grief, and similar states, which seem
to be genuinely unpleasant, are yet not considered altogether valueless. It is from just this fact that many
infer that the true standard of value, according to
which not every pain is valueless, and not every pleasure
valuable, must be other than pleasure.

We consider these points in turn:

(1) The cause of the evil repute of the word "pleasure," or related terms, lies, in my opinion, only in those
mutual human influences which can in the widest
sense be called "education."

All education concerns the transformation of man,
the alteration of his dispositions; it consists in the
strengthening or forming of certain impulses, and the
weakening or removal of others. That is (cf. the
definition of impulse in Chapter III), education attempts to equip certain ideas with a greater pleasure-
tone and to make others, on the contrary, have as little

as possible, or even to make them very unpleasant. In education as it actually takes place (and I speak not only of the education of children, but of every moral influence exerted by men upon one another) the second, negative, method which tries to repress and dam up the existing impulses is used preponderantly. It has indeed long been a reasonable demand of pedagogy to prefer the positive method, to strengthen and develop the desirable impulses, instead of spending all energy upon overcoming the undesirable; but this latter method is much easier, and it is also usually considered more urgent first to protect society from injuries that can come to it from the unbridled impulses of its members; the cultivation of useful dispositions is carried on only secondarily. Therefore it happens that education for the most part works by means of restrictions and prohibitions; the state, for example, sanctions its laws by means of punishments for transgression alone, not by means of rewards for obedience. And thus we explain the fact, to which attention was called in the beginning of Chapter IV, that our whole morality exhibits in such high degree a *prohibitory* character.

The essence of prohibition consists in the fact that we are told, "You must not do what you would like to do." Something, the idea of which is originally pleasant, is declared to be bad by the moral precept; and the impression arises that in general what brings pleasure is always bad. The fact that for the most part I come in contact with moral rules and educative measures only when someone wishes to *change* something in me

(otherwise they would not be required) has the consequence that what is commanded by morality always
appears to be what one would not do of one's own self,
naturally. I am firmly convinced that this is the
correct, startlingly simple explanation of the fact that
nature and morality appear to many philosophers as
opposites, that Kant believes it necessary to distinguish
between man as a natural creature and man as morally
rational, that for Fichte virtue is nothing but the "overcoming of outer and inner nature," that James defines
moral conduct as that which proceeds in the line of
greatest resistance (while conversely, nature follows the
principle of least resistance). According to these
theories the moral is never the natural, and morality is
never self-evident.

How clearly we now see through the psychology of
all those philosophers who reject pleasure as the standard of value! Morality, in order to attain its ends,
must remove the pleasure-tone from certain ideas, tear
away their seductive finery, put desired goals in a bad
light, make alluring ones appear suspicious. How
easily it can happen that in this process of exerting
moral influence the peculiar purpose and meaning of
morality is seen, even though it is really only instrumental. Although at first it never occurred to morality to abhor pleasure as such, must it not almost necessarily come, habitually, to treat pleasure as something
better avoided, as something dangerous, low, and common? But if pleasure is the only value, indeed if it is
valuable at all, morality could not possibly warn

against all possible satisfactions; hence pleasure must be something disreputable. However, it was not noticed that originally no moral precept ever warned against pleasure as such, but always only against definite activities or objects which were pleasant. Yet if a child is constantly warned against poisonous mushrooms, must it not in the end fear all mushrooms and hold them always in suspicion; even though the warning ultimately did not concern mushrooms, but only poison?

Not that moral teachers have never made a clear distinction between valuable and evil pleasures, between permissible and unpermissible joys. For they have used the principle of reward also, and the pleasure that serves as the reward must of course be "good." But it is, again, very characteristic that especially in religions the tendency, at least, existed to banish as many as possible of the *natural* feelings of pleasure to the realm of prohibited things; so that this realm in the case of the extremists, the ascetics, finally included all natural pleasure. Thus arises the opposition of "earthly" and "heavenly" joys; the former are all worthless, only the other-worldly joys are good. It would be the task of a sensible education to return the heavenly joys to earth again.

Who knows whether moral sermons, by means of suggestion, have not given the impulse to many a pessimism, which in turn easily found further reasons for the worthlessness of pleasure, for example, that every joy contains within itself the germ of future sorrow, just because, perhaps, every pleasure must end, and this is always painful.

The modern philosopher of value does not go so far as to consider value and pleasure as opposites, but he supports the suggestion of the moralist in so far as he grants to pleasure no *moral* value, and therefore rejects it entirely as a standard of value. I repeat that this view is explained in a very large part simply by the method of moral education, which must declare so many pleasant things to be reprehensible, and thereby brings pleasure as such into disrepute.

3. *Happiness and Sorrow as Mixed States*

(2) The consideration of the second explanatory ground of that view leads us to more weighty matters. This second reason lies, we noted, in the fact that in our judgments on the value of a life we do not at all rate the unpleasant experiences, pain and sorrow, only negatively. We believe on the contrary that they *can* at least serve to give to life that richness which is presupposed by the highest value. For what kind of life do we call the most valuable? Is it not that to which we ascribe nobility and greatness? And do not these words mean something altogether different from a maximum of pleasure? Again and again we hear that if one strives for greatness he must renounce happiness. "The fate of the great men of history has not been happy," says Hegel. If it is true that the highest in life cannot exist without sorrow and pain, then, so it

seems, pleasure is not simply the valuable, but must give up its rank as the standard of value to something altogether different.

Everyone feels that behind such objections there stands some kind of serious and significant truth, and that superficial arguments will be of no avail against it. Such would be an argument which said that a life of nobility and greatness is in fact valuable only for *others* who profit by the deeds of the genius; those who enjoy his achievements value and praise his life. But for himself it has actually little value; unless an excessive desire for power and ambition is thus satisfied in him, whereby compensation is made for the burdens he took upon himself.

This argument is invalid: in the first place because the nobility and moral greatness of a human life is not always measured by successful deeds, that is, according to its social utility; and, in the second place, because the great man himself, even without desire for power and fame, can feel the value of an heroic existence so strongly that despite his "unhappiness" he would change with no one to whom life's joys came in a less adulterated form.

Thus it requires more penetrating considerations to see whether the situations described do not require us to revise our view of the nature of value. What we have to do is, again, only this, to ask: "What is the actual meaning of the words like 'happiness' and 'sorrow' in those cases where a 'higher' but sorrowful life is contrasted with a 'lower' but happy one, and praised as the more valuable?"

The word "happiness" has in any case such a vague meaning that in different contexts very different things are meant. The same holds, moreover, of the Greek term εὐδαιμονία, while, for example, the Latin *beatitudo* has a more definite coloring, corresponding to the German *Seligkeit*. In the polemic against the eudaemonistic way of thinking, the vague expression "happiness" is commonly understood as if it meant something like enjoyment, comfort, gratification. These words also, of course, having little of the exactness of scientific terms. The cited aphorism from Hegel, on the happiness of the great men of history, continues, "They never attain peaceful enjoyment!" Is the assertion that a noble life is more valuable than a happy one to say only that greatness is incompatible with "peaceful enjoyment"? This would gladly be granted, even by him who holds that greatness and happiness are not mutually exclusive, and who is of the opinion that all nobility finally depends upon some feelings of pleasure; he need only deny the identification of happiness with peaceful enjoyment, and remember that the strongest feelings of pleasure are connected with other states than "peaceful enjoyment." And he would certainly be right!

But in this way only a very crude difficulty would be overcome. The question troubling us would still be far from settled. Granted human nature and conditions of life to be what they are, it must be admitted that a human life can become more valuable through sorrow. Thus suffering must be valuable either directly or indirectly, that is, either contain pleasure itself or constitute the necessary condition of it. Otherwise the statement cannot be validly maintained that value is determined by pleasure alone. Is anything like this possible?

It seems to be impossible only so long as we forget that happiness and sorrow are terms of very indefinite meaning, and therefore need not at all coincide with the pair of concepts pleasure, pain, which we assume as strictly defined psychologically, and use with a constant meaning. Dostoevsky, who certainly did not reflect less than other men on the value of life, puts into the mouth of one of his heroes the question (in *Letters from the Underworld*), "What is better, cheap happiness or noble sorrow?" And he considers the answer to be so self-evident that he neglects to give it, but has the hero repeat, "Well, which is better?" Here, there is added to the words "sorrow" and "happiness" an adjective that would result in a contradiction in terms if by happiness were meant something wholly pleasant, and by sorrow pure pain. For "cheap" is a disparaging description here: what is thus described must show some speck of pain on its otherwise brilliant garb; and conversely, so long as a sorrow can still be "noble" it is not a *pure* pain, but still bears some bright star on its dark raiment. On the other hand, Dostoevsky also obviously uses the word "happiness" in its *pure* meaning of *beatitudo*; in *The Brothers Kara-mazov* he has the old man, Zosima, say, "For men are made for happiness. Whoever is completely happy is worthy to say to himself: I have fulfilled God's will on this earth. All teachers, all saints, all saintly martyrs have been happy." Thus it is clear (and with the extreme complexity of life really self-evident) that words like "happiness," "unhappiness," "pleasure," "sorrow" are used in life and poetry for complex states having mixed components of feeling. The psychologist, who by his analysis must expose those *pure* tones which he calls "pleasure" and "pain," deals with abstractions and arrives at formulations which must appear paradoxical. (The law of motivation enunciated in Chapter II, and the reduction of all value to pleasure are such formulations.) When even such an elementary sensation as pain can, according to the circumstances, possess pleasant as well as unpleasant components it is no wonder that more complicated psychic states have a structure even more difficult to discover.

From considerations such as these we form the conjecture that "suffering," when it is valued positively and viewed as a desirable constituent of life, designates without exception a compounded state (or better, structurally complicated, for in the true sense nothing psychic is "compounded"), in which the psychologist can point out the feeling components that are to be made responsible for the "value."

4. *Associative Pleasure in Sorrow*

We speak first of the simple, almost trivial case, that a state which "in itself" (that is, under usual conditions, and without special relation to past and future things) is unpleasant obtains a pleasure component because it is associated with ideas which are strongly colored by pleasure. They have this coloring either because they relate to previously had joyful experiences, or because they relate to future states which are pictured as joyful. Everyone can easily find hundreds of examples in his own experience for each of these cases. To the first sort belong all those in which an ugly object is cherished because cheerful memories are joined to it, or where for the same reason various unpleasant sensations lose their unpleasantness; even bad odors are sometimes valued. I once heard of a worker who was in the habit of opening a gas-cock to enjoy the odor; he had been employed in a gas-plant and had evidently had a pleasant time there.

We have cases of the second sort wherever one undertakes a painful performance for the sake of its effects; the idea of these makes the activity pleasant. To very many persons all "labor" seems to be of this sort. Conversely, every overcoming of difficulty easily comes to be considered unpleasant, as a mere means to an end, which it need not in the least be (this observation is important for the valuation of an "heroic" life).

But above all we should think of what in the widest

sense can be called a promise or a threat, reward or punishment. Every pleasure can be called a reward if it characterizes a state which is the effect of definite behavior, and has the consequence that the idea of this result, and thereby the behavior leading to it, itself becomes pleasant. The representation of that future state is then called "hope," and there are doubtless but few states of intensive pleasure in human life to which feelings of hope do not somehow contribute. Perhaps in general, hope (longing is related to it) is the source of the happiest feelings. If we should destroy them, so that of every pleasure only the momentary present component remained, so to speak, this would at least be a pretty wretched remainder. This fact alone appears to render unjustified the attitude of those moralists and philosophers who look disdainfully upon the principle of reward or compensation, who see but a very crude method in its application, and who reject entirely the fact that it is used in ethics to locate the value of suffering, also only in part, in the reward for suffering. This is, on the contrary, a correct explanation. That it is so simple does not justify us in rejecting it as a superficial eudaemonistic construction.

That eudaemonistic explanations are considered superficial, even immoral, can be understood from the considerations of the first part of this chapter. For the same reason one seeks to defend the religions, especially Christianity, against the charge of exhibiting eudaemonistic tendencies in arousing other-worldly hope. But this seems to me to be altogether useless and superfluous. It is not true that reference to compensation by future happiness for suffering is incompatible with true magnanimity, or indicates an appeal to "egoism" (cf. Chapter III); consolation and reward are much rather the expression of kindness. And kindness too is noble. Some of the most beautiful passages of the Gospels owe their beauty to the subjoined promises: "Blessed are they which are persecuted for righteousness' sake, for theirs is the kingdom of heaven." Often it is the references to future joys alone that give even the formulations of moral precepts their grandeur, by placing men in relationships affording wide perspectives in which things assume their proper value. The "Judge not!" obtains its force only from the added phrase, "That ye be not judged."

5. *Is Sorrow a Necessary Condition of Pleasure?*

Hitherto we have dealt only with the simple (but nevertheless important) idea that suffering is valuable whenever it represents the path to joy; the valuation of the end being carried over to the means, according to well-known laws. We might now attempt to generalize this thought to the more important observation that the path to joy *always* leads through suffering, that they are connected by a law of nature.

This law could only be the law of *contrast*, and it would in this case say that never-ending states of pleasure could not be felt as such (thus really would not be such) unless they were interrupted by pain: as, for example, the Pythagoreans supposed that we did not hear the music of the spheres, solely because they sounded a continuous monotone. Pleasure would only be possible after antecedent pain.

This inference is erroneous, even though the law of contrast holds. To be sure, we would never speak of the value of health if there were no illness; praises of spring would not be sung if it did not follow winter, and if the whole year rounded out equably; but from this it only follows that some *change* is necessary if lively feelings are to occur. Just as winter is not merely a miserable season but has its own joys, though *different* from those of summer, so it would suffice if different qualities of pleasure alternated with each other, or if states of highest joy followed indifferent or mildly pleasant ones; the former would stand out from the latter quite well enough. Thus the necessity of pain as the pre-condition of pleasure cannot be deduced in this manner. At most one could say that the transition from a joyful to a less joyful state is under all conditions painful; but then the observation again becomes trivial and does not solve our real problem.

Hence, even though here we cannot offer a proof, it still seems to be a fact of experience (I am of course not altogether sure of it) that the most profound joys of life are actually not possible unless, previously, grave feelings of pain have been experienced. It seems that the soul requires them in order to become receptive of the sublimest pleasures. This would indeed be a deplorable fact, and not one we would want to palliate

by saying that it is not in the least deplorable.   But, if
it really exists, then we should understand better why
a human life can attain its highest value only by passing through the extremes.   A life such as the modest
poet Mörike prayed for:

> *Wollest mit Freuden*
> *Und wollest mit Leiden*
> *Mich nicht überschütten!*
> *—doch in der Mitten*
> *Liegt holdes Bescheiden. . . .*[1]

could not be truly great, not because it lacked the deep-
est suffering, but because of the absence of the greatest
joys, the path to which seems indeed to lead only
through pain.

6. *The Bliss of Suffering*

The value which, thus far, we have been able to assign to "suffering" was not inherent in it, but accrued
to it only to the extent to which it was a means to pleasant ends.   Is this the only kind of value that is to be
found in it?   Does it explain adequately the feeling,
which upon deeper reflection one can hardly resist, that
suffering has the important function in life of protect-
ing it from "shallowness," where shallowness is the opposite of "depth," a word by which one certainly wishes
to designate what is most valuable in life?   It seems to

---

[1] [Let me not be overwhelmed with joys and with sorrows,
for gentle moderation lies in the mean. . . .]

me that what we have hitherto discovered is insufficient to do justice to these matters. Consequently we are faced by the question of whether there is not either a value wholly independent of pleasure, or whether in the states called "sorrowful" there are not still to be found some pleasure components, which belong there by their very nature, as it were, and are not introduced by a comparatively external association.

I shall say at once that in my opinion the word "suffer," in its significant sense, is always used only for mixed states, for complicated experiences whose feeling tones are never wholly and purely pain. We remarked earlier that emotions of wholly unmixed pain are rare, and occur only in the cases of unmitigated aversion and disgust. It is only an end with such accompanying affects that can never be willed; and this with the necessity of a natural law (cf. Chapter II). Most forms of disagreeable things tend to have a hidden pleasure component, as it were, and this holds even of anger, fear, care, and of mourning. Even the profound grief with which we stand at the deathbed of a loved one is permeated by the peculiar remote sweetness from which the thought of death is seldom free, and upon which perhaps rests the feeling of its sublimity.

Such involved states, by virtue of their richer structure, naturally constitute the field of poetry. There the bliss of sorrow is praised again and again, and if the poet longs for bitterness (Heine) it is the sweetness of bitterness which makes it an object of ardent desire. Where this problem becomes most clearly visible is in tragedy. Since Aristotle, ever new attempts have been made to explain the pleasure in tragedy, and the explanations remain unsatisfying so long as they (as did that of Aristotle) refer the joy in the tragic to subsequent associations. The pleasure lies rather in part in "suffering" itself, and for *this* component the catharsis and reconciliation, whose role in tragedy may otherwise be great enough, is no longer necessary. Thus Gerhart Hauptmann in *Michael Kramer* says, "Even what serves to humble us is at once glorious and terrible."

It has in general not escaped the notice of the poets that experiences of "suffering" are not wholly disagreeable, not altogether painful; and they have often in their manner expressed this, saying that joy and sorrow are in essence related. In Anatole France we read (*La Vie en Fleur,* the end), *"On aime aussi la vie, la douloureuse vie, parcequ'on aime la douleur. Et comment ne l'aimerait on pas? Elle ressemble à la joie, et parfois se confond avec elle."* [2]

We have now to formulate that fact or to discover that general truth which lies at the base of such statements as the one just cited. What lies behind the "similarity" of pleasure and sorrow, here affirmed?

According to the established method of psychology, we shall consider for the solution of our problem the *external* mode of appearance of the effect, the behavior

---

[2] [One loves life also, sorrowful life, because one loves sorrow. And why shouldn't one love it? It resembles joy, and is sometimes confused with it.]

exhibited by a joyful and a suffering person. And at once it strikes us that in addition to differences there are very remarkable agreements to be observed. It is very significant that suffering and great joy have in common in their expression such a pronounced phenomenon as *tears*. *"Les haut plaisirs sont ceux qui font presque pleurer"* [3] (Guyau, *Vers d'un Philosophe*, p. 139). A man weeps when he suffers, and tears come to his eyes when he experiences great joy, even (and this is important for us) in the presence of a noble deed, or when he hears of a generous reconciliation; in short, whenever he has elevated "ethical" feelings. Pure pain (the feeling of something repulsive, or simply offensive) brings no tears; we do not weep, but scream or groan when in great pain (*Laokoon*).

What is common to the joyful and sorrowful situations in which men weep? Evidently a powerful convulsion of man's whole nature, in which, however, the force is not the decisive thing, but rather the fact that the *whole* person is affected to a depth which very few impressions can reach. These are of course only figurative expressions. Translated into the language of psychology, they state that in such powerful experiences we have to do with certain functions of the soul (one can also say "physiological functions" without altering the sense) which can be aroused in the most diverse ways, but which are very difficult to arouse, and which for the volitional life have a fundamental significance; so that its character has an essential dependence upon

---

[3] [The great pleasures are those that nearly make us weep.]

them.   They are made active by pleasant as well as unpleasant powerful stimuli; but this activity itself is always pleasant.   These functions constitute something
elevated and great in men in the double sense that their
power in the psychic life is enormous, and that they are
the source of very intense joys.   Moments in which
one becomes aware of their activity are moments of
exalted feeling.   Apart from certain exceptions, every
vehement psychic process, every deployment of power,
and lively activity is pleasant.   If, however, the process penetrates to the depths of the soul one has feelings
of sublimity ranging from a transitory "touching" emotion to the highest unwavering inspiration, observable
in world-shaking deeds.

Perhaps, for obscure reasons, suffering rather than
joy has the power of moving the soul to its inmost
depths—pain stirring it as a sharp plow turns the soil.
(The word "pathos," which we use approximately
with the meaning of "inspiration," actually means "suffering.")   If this were true, we should better understand why suffering is so eloquently praised as something great and holy, and why the poet believed that
heavenly powers reveal themselves in it:

> *Wer nie sein Brot mit Tränen ass,*
> *wer nie die kummervollen Nächte*
> *auf seinem Bette weinend sass,*
> *der kennt euch nicht, ihr himmlischen Mächte!* [4]
>
> (Goethe)

---

[4] [Who has not eaten his bread in tears, nor sat weeping on
his bed through nights of misery, knows ye not, ye heavenly
powers!]

But I believe that one could with the same justification say (and Goethe also would willingly have said) that who does not know the heavenly powers has never experienced the ecstasies of pure joy. Nietzsche was probably right in his aphorism that pleasure is profounder than affliction. Indeed there is no essential reason, and our considerations led to none, why intense joys alone should not suffice for us to rise to true greatness, to reach the ultimate depths of our nature, and to attain all of the sublimities of life. That suffering more easily succeeds in stirring the soul into great convulsion, making it ready for the highest joys, is probably connected with the fact that in general the most intense pains yield the strongest impulses. A painful state obviously presses more violently toward a change than does a pleasant one. We run most rapidly when escaping a danger, more easily, however, when striving to reach a goal. Then we enjoy the effort itself and are not in a hurry. Thus it happens that great art derives more readily from sorrow than from pleasure, that almost all the great artists have also suffered greatly.

Der Lorbeerkranz ist, wo er dir erscheint,
Ein Zeichen mehr des Leidens als des Glücks.[5]
(Goethe, *Tasso*)

The sufferer calls more force into play, he is more in need of the work of art, which liberates him and brings salvation.

---

[5] [The laurel-wreath . . . is a symbol more of sorrow than of happiness.]

If in this manner pain releases the strongest psychic powers, still it is no law of nature that intense joy could not do the same; and experience teaches that this actually happens, though examples of it are rarer. We must in any case desire that they become more frequent; nor is there visible reason why, with advancing civilization, development should not take place along this line. Indeed, perhaps true progress in civilization consists in just this, that suffering become more and more unnecessary for the release of powerful pleasure-bringing forces, this role being taken over more and more by joyful inspiration, as we observe it occasionally in especially favored men.

———

In this chapter we have reached the following results: the opinion that pleasure is often not, or not at all, valuable rests upon a certain prejudice whose origin has been disclosed and which has thus been rendered harmless. The opinion that "suffering" is valuable is correct, but only because the generally very complex state designated by this word is always shot through with certain feelings of pleasure to which the value can be referred. What holds of sorrow holds *a fortiori* of all other things, that is, they owe their value to the joy they promise, which is the only measure of their value.

CHAPTER VII

When Is a Man Responsible?

1. *The Pseudo-Problem of Freedom of the Will*

With hesitation and reluctance I prepare to add this chapter to the discussion of ethical problems. For in it I must speak of a matter which, even at present, is thought to be a fundamental ethical question, but which got into ethics and has become a much discussed problem only because of a misunderstanding. This is the so-called problem of the freedom of the will. Moreover, this pseudo-problem has long since been settled by the efforts of certain sensible persons; and, above all, the state of affairs just described has been often disclosed—with exceptional clarity by Hume. Hence it is really one of the greatest scandals of philosophy that again and again so much paper and printer's ink is devoted to this matter, to say nothing of the expenditure of thought, which could have been applied to more important problems (assuming that it would have sufficed for these). Thus I should truly be ashamed to write a chapter on "freedom." In the chapter heading, the word "responsible" indicates what concerns ethics, and designates the point at which mis-

understanding arises. Therefore the concept of responsibility constitutes our theme, and if in the process
of its clarification I also must speak of the concept of
freedom I shall, of course, say only what others have
already said better; consoling myself with the thought
that in this way alone can anything be done to put an
end at last to that scandal.

The main task of ethics (of which we convinced ourselves in Chapter I) is to explain moral behavior. To
explain means to refer back to laws: every science, including psychology, is possible only in so far as there
are such laws to which the events can be referred.
Since the assumption that *all* events are subject to universal laws is called the principle of causality, one can
also say, "Every science presupposes the principle of
causality." Therefore every explanation of human behavior must also assume the validity of causal laws; in
this case the existence of psychological laws. (If for
example our law of motivation of Chapter II were incorrect, then human conduct would be quite unex-
plained.) All of our experience strengthens us in the
belief that this presupposition is realized, at least to the
extent required for all purposes of practical life in in-
tercourse with nature and human beings, and also for
the most precise demands of technique. Whether, indeed, the principle of causality holds universally,
whether, that is, *determinism* is true, we do not know;
no one knows. But we do know that it is impossible
to settle the dispute between determinism and indeterminism by mere reflection and speculation, by the con-

sideration of so many reasons for and so many reasons against (which collectively and individually are but pseudo-reasons). Such an attempt becomes especially ridiculous when one considers with what enormous expenditure of experimental and logical skill contemporary physics carefully approaches the question of whether causality can be maintained for the most minute intra-atomic events.

But the dispute concerning "freedom of the will" generally proceeds in such fashion that its advocates attempt to refute, and its opponents to prove, the validity of the causal principle, both using hackneyed arguments, and neither in the least abashed by the magnitude of the undertaking. (I can exclude only Bergson from this criticism, with whom, however, this whole question is not an ethical but a metaphysical problem. His ideas, which in my opinion will not stand epistemological analysis, are of no significance for us.) Others distinguish two realms, in one of which determinism holds, but not in the other. This line of thought (which was unfortunately taken by Kant) is, however, quite the most worthless (though Schopenhauer considered it to be Kant's most profound idea).

Fortunately, it is not necessary to lay claim to a final solution of the causal problem in order to say what is necessary in ethics concerning responsibility; there is required only an analysis of the concept, the careful determination of the meaning which is in fact joined to the words "responsibility" and "freedom" as these are actually used. If men had made clear to themselves the sense of those propositions, which we use in everyday life, that pseudo-argument which lies at the root of the pseudo-problem, and which recurs thousands of times within and outside of philosophical books, would never have arisen.

The argument runs as follows: "If determinism is true, if, that is, all events obey immutable laws, then my will too is always determined, by my innate character and my motives.   Hence my decisions are necessary, not free.   But if so, then I am not responsible for my acts, for I would be accountable for them only if I could do something about the way my decisions went; but I can do nothing about it, since they proceed with necessity from my character and the motives.   And I have made neither, and have no power over them: the motives come from without, and my character is the necessary product of the innate tendencies and the external influences which have been effective during my lifetime.   Thus determinism and moral responsibility are incompatible. Moral responsibility presupposes freedom, that is, exemption from causality."

This process of reasoning rests upon a whole series of confusions, just as the links of a chain hang together. We must show these confusions to be such, and thus destroy them.

2. Two Meanings of the Word "Law"

It all begins with an erroneous interpretation of the meaning of "law."   In practice this is understood as a rule by which the state prescribes certain behavior to its citizens. These rules often contradict the natural desires of the citizens (for if they did not do so, there would be no reason for making them), and are in fact not followed by many of them; while others obey, but under *compulsion*. The state does in fact compel its citizens by imposing certain sanctions (punishments) which serve to bring their desires into harmony with the prescribed laws.

In natural science, on the other hand, the word "law" means something quite different. The natural law is not a *pre*scription as to how something should behave, but a formula, a *de*scription of how something does in fact behave. The two forms of "laws" have only this in common: both tend to be expressed in *formulae*. Otherwise they have absolutely nothing to do with one another, and it is very blameworthy that the same word has been used for two such different things; but even more so that philosophers have allowed themselves to be led into serious errors by this usage. Since natural laws are only descriptions of what happens, there can be in regard to them no talk of "compulsion." The laws of celestial mechanics do not prescribe to the planets how they have to move, as though the planets would actually like to move quite otherwise, and are only forced by these burdensome laws of Kepler to move in orderly paths; no, these laws do not in any way "compel" the planets, but express only what in fact planets actually do.

If we apply this to volition, we are enlightened at

once, even before the other confusions are discovered. When we say that a man's will "obeys psychological laws," these are not civic laws, which compel him to make certain decisions, or dictate desires to him, which he would in fact prefer not to have. They are laws of nature, merely expressing which desires he *actually has* under given conditions; they describe the nature of the will in the same manner as the astronomical laws describe the nature of planets. "Compulsion" occurs where man is prevented from realizing his natural desires. How could the rule according to which these natural desires arise itself be considered as "compulsion"?

3. *Compulsion and Necessity*

But this is the second confusion to which the first leads almost inevitably: after conceiving the laws of nature, anthropomorphically, as order imposed *nolens volens* upon the events, one adds to them the concept of "necessity." This word, derived from "need," also comes to us from practice, and is used there in the sense of inescapable compulsion. To apply the word with this meaning to natural laws is of course senseless, for the presupposition of an opposing desire is lacking; and it is then confused with something altogether different, which is actually an attribute of natural laws. That is, universality. It is of the essence of natural laws to be universally valid, for only when we have found a rule which holds of events without exception do we *call* the rule a law of nature. Thus when we say "a natural law holds necessarily" this has but one legitimate meaning: "It holds in *all* cases where it is applicable." It is again very deplorable that the word "necessary" has been applied to natural laws (or, what amounts to the same thing, with reference to causality), for it is quite superfluous, since the expression "universally valid" is available. Universal validity is something altogether different from "compulsion"; these concepts belong to spheres so remote from each other that once insight into the error has been gained one can no longer conceive the possibility of a confusion.

The confusion of two concepts always carries with it the confusion of their contradictory opposites. The opposite of the universal validity of a formula, of the existence of a law, is the nonexistence of a law, indeterminism, acausality; while the opposite of compulsion is what in practice everyone calls "freedom." Here emerges the nonsense, trailing through centuries, that freedom means "exemption from the causal principle," or "not subject to the laws of nature." Hence it is believed necessary to vindicate indeterminism in order to save human freedom.

4. *Freedom and Indeterminism*

This is quite mistaken. Ethics has, so to speak, no moral interest in the purely theoretical question of "determinism or indeterminism?," but only a theoretical interest, namely: in so far as it seeks the laws of conduct, and can find them only to the extent that causality holds.   But the question of whether man is morally free (that is, has that freedom which, as we shall show, is the presupposition of moral responsibility) is altogether different from the problem of determinism. Hume was especially clear on this point. He indicated the inadmissible confusion of the concepts of "indeterminism" and "freedom"; but he retained, inappropriately, the word "freedom" for both, calling the one freedom of "the will," the other, genuine kind, "freedom of conduct." He showed that morality is interested only in the latter, and that such freedom, in general, is unquestionably to be attributed to mankind. And this is quite correct.   Freedom means the opposite of compulsion; a man is *free* if he does not act under *compulsion,* and he is compelled or unfree when he is hindered from without in the realization of his natural desires.   Hence he is unfree when he is locked up, or chained, or when someone forces him at the point of a gun to do what otherwise he would not do.   This is quite clear, and everyone will admit that the everyday or legal notion of the lack of freedom is thus correctly interpreted, and that a man will be considered quite free and responsible if no such external compulsion is exerted upon him.   There are certain cases which lie between these clearly described ones, as, say, when someone acts under the influence of alcohol or a narcotic.   In such cases we consider the man to be more or less unfree, and hold him less accountable, because we rightly view the influence of the drug as "external," even though it is found within the body; it prevents him from making decisions in the manner peculiar to his nature. If he takes the narcotic of his own will, we make him completely responsible for *this* act and transfer a part of the responsibility to the consequences, making, as it were, an average or mean condemnation of the whole. In the case also of a person who is mentally ill we do not consider him free with respect to those acts in which the disease expresses itself, because we view the illness as a disturbing factor which hinders the normal functioning of his natural tendencies. We make not him but his disease responsible.

5. *The Nature of Responsibility*

But what does this really signify? What do we mean by this concept of responsibility which goes along with that of "freedom," and which plays such an important role in morality? It is easy to attain complete clarity in this matter; we need only carefully determine the manner in which the concept is used. What is the case in practice when we impute "responsibility" to a person? What is our aim in doing this? The judge has to discover who is responsible for a given act in order that he may *punish* him. We are inclined to be less concerned with the inquiry as to who deserves *reward* for an act, and we have no special officials for this; but of course the principle would be the same. But let us stick to punishment in order to make the idea clear. What is punishment, actually? The view still often expressed, that it is a natural *retaliation* for past wrong, ought no longer to be defended in cultivated society; for the opinion that an increase in sorrow can be "made good again" by further sorrow is altogether barbarous. Certainly the origin of punishment may lie in an impulse of retaliation or vengeance; but what is such an impulse except the instinctive desire to destroy the *cause* of the deed to be avenged, by the destruction of or injury to the malefactor? Punishment is concerned only with the institution of causes, of *motives* of conduct, and this alone is its meaning. Punishment is an educative measure, and as such is a means to the formation of motives, which are in part to prevent the wrongdoer from repeating the act (reformation) and in part to prevent others from committing a similar act (intimidation). Analogously, in the case of reward we are concerned with an incentive.

Hence the question regarding responsibility is the question: Who, in a given case, is to be punished? Who is to be considered the true wrongdoer? This problem is not identical with that regarding the original instigator of the act; for the great-grandparents of the man, from whom he inherited his character, might in the end be the cause, or the statesmen who are responsible for his social milieu, and so forth. But the "doer" is the one *upon whom the motive must have acted* in order, with certainty, to have prevented the act (or called it forth, as the case may be). Considera-

tion of remote causes is of no help here, for in the first
place their actual contribution cannot be determined,
and in the second place they are generally out of reach.
Rather, we must find the person in whom the decisive
junction of causes lies. The question of who is responsible is the question concerning the *correct point
of application of the motive*. And the important thing
is that in this its meaning is completely exhausted; behind it there lurks no mysterious connection between
transgression and requital, which is merely *indicated*
by the described state of affairs. It is a matter only of
knowing who is to be punished or rewarded, in order
that punishment and reward function as such—be able
to achieve their goal.

Thus, all the facts connected with the concepts of
responsibility and imputation are at once made intelligible. We do not charge an insane person with responsibility, for the very reason that he offers no unified point for the application of a motive. It would
be pointless to try to affect him by means of promises
or threats, when his confused soul fails to respond to
such influence because its normal mechanism is out of
order. We do not try to give him motives, but try to
heal him (metaphorically, we make his sickness responsible, and try to remove its causes). When a man
is forced by threats to commit certain acts we do not
blame him, but the one who held the pistol at his
breast. The reason is clear: the act would have been
prevented had we been able to restrain the person who

threatened him; and this person is the one whom we must influence in order to prevent similar acts in the future.

6. *The Consciousness of Responsibility*

But much more important than the question of when a man is said to be responsible is that of when he *himself* feels responsible.   Our whole treatment would be untenable if it gave no explanation of this.   It is, then, a welcome confirmation of the view here developed that the subjective feeling of responsibility coincides with the objective judgment.   It is a fact of experience that, in general, the person blamed or condemned is conscious of the fact that he was "rightly" taken to account—of course, under the supposition that no error has been made, that the assumed state of affairs actually occurred.   What is this consciousness of having been the true doer of the act, the actual instigator? Evidently not merely that it was he who took the steps required for its performance; but there must be added the awareness that he did it "independently," "of his own initiative," or however it be expressed.   This feeling is simply the consciousness of *freedom,* which is merely the knowledge of having acted of one's *own* desires.   And "one's own desires" are those which have their origin in the regularity of one's character in the given situation, and are not imposed by an external power, as explained above.   The absence of the external power expresses itself in the well-known feeling (usually considered characteristic of the consciousness of freedom) *that one could also have acted otherwise.* How this indubitable experience ever came to be an argument in favor of indeterminism is incomprehensible to me. It is of course obvious that I should have acted differently had I *willed* something else; but the feeling never says that I could also have willed something else, even though this is true, if, that is, other motives had been present. And it says even less that under *exactly the same* inner and outer conditions I could also have willed something else. How could such a feeling inform me of anything regarding the purely theoretical question of whether the principle of causality holds or not? Of course, after what has been said on the subject, I do not undertake to demonstrate the principle, but I do deny that from any such fact of consciousness the least follows regarding the principle's validity. This feeling is not the consciousness of the absence of a cause, but of something altogether different, namely, of *freedom,* which consists in the fact that I can act as I desire.

Thus the feeling of responsibility assumes that I acted freely, that my own desires impelled me; and if because of this feeling I willingly suffer blame for my behavior or reproach myself, and thereby admit that I might have acted otherwise, this means that other behavior was compatible with the laws of volition—of course, granted other motives. And I myself desire the existence of such motives and bear the pain (regret and sorrow) caused me by my behavior so that its repetition will be prevented. To blame oneself means just to apply motives of improvement to oneself, which is usually the task of the educator. But if, for example, one does something under the influence of torture, feelings of guilt and regret are absent, for one knows that according to the laws of volition no other behavior was possible—no matter what ideas, because of their feeling tones, might have functioned as motives. The important thing, always, is that the feeling of responsibility means the realization that one's self, one's own psychic processes constitute the point at which motives must be applied in order to govern the acts of one's body.

7. *Causality as the Presupposition of Responsibility*

We can speak of motives only in a causal context; thus it becomes clear how very much the concept of responsibility rests upon that of causation, that is, upon the regularity of volitional decisions. In fact if we should conceive of a decision as utterly without any cause (this would in all strictness be the indeterministic presupposition) then the act would be entirely a matter of *chance,* for chance is identical with the absence of a cause; there is no other opposite of causality. Could we under such conditions make the agent responsible? Certainly not. Imagine a man, always calm, peaceful and blameless, who suddenly falls upon and begins to beat a stranger. He is held and questioned regarding the motive of his action, to which he answers, in his opinion truthfully, as we assume: "There was no motive for my behavior.

Try as I may I can discover no reason. My volition was without any cause—I desired to do so, and there is simply nothing else to be said about it." We should shake our heads and call him insane, because we have to believe that there was a cause, and lacking any other we must assume some mental disturbance as the only cause remaining; but certainly no one would hold him to be responsible. If decisions were causeless there would be no sense in trying to influence men; and we see at once that this is the reason why we could not bring such a man to account, but would always have only a shrug of the shoulders in answer to his behavior. One can easily determine that in practice we make an agent the more responsible the more motives we can find for his conduct. If a man guilty of an atrocity was an enemy of his victim, if previously he had shown violent tendencies, if some special circumstance angered him, then we impose severe punishment upon him; while the fewer the reasons to be found for an offense the less do we condemn the agent, but make "unlucky chance," a momentary aberration, or something of the sort, responsible. We do not find the causes of misconduct in his character, and therefore we do not try to influence it for the better: this and only this is the significance of the fact that we do not put the responsibility upon him. And he too feels this to be so, and says, "I cannot understand how such a thing could have happened to me."

In general we know very well how to discover the causes of conduct in the characters of our fellow men; and how to use this knowledge in the prediction of their future behavior, often with as much certainty as that with which we know that a lion and a rabbit will behave quite differently in the same situation. From all this it is evident that in practice no one thinks of questioning the principle of causality, that, thus, the attitude of the practical man offers no excuse to the metaphysician for confusing freedom from compulsion with the absence of a cause. If one makes clear to himself that a causeless happening is identical with a chance happening, and that, consequently, an indetermined will would destroy all responsibility, then every desire will cease which might be father to an indeterministic thought. No one can prove determinism, but it is certain that we assume its validity in all of our practical life, and that in particular we can apply the concept of responsibility to human conduct only in so far as the causal principle holds of volitional processes.

For a final clarification I bring together again a list of those concepts which tend, in the traditional treatment of the "problem of freedom," to be confused. In the place of the concepts on the left are put, mistakenly, those of the right, and those in the vertical order form a chain, so that sometimes the previous confusion is the cause of that which follows:

Natural Law.	Law of State.
Determinism (Causality).	Compulsion.
(Universal Validity).	(Necessity).
Indeterminism (Chance).	Freedom.
(No Cause).	(No Compulsion).

CHAPTER VIII

What Paths Lead to Value?

Prepared by the questions already asked, and, let us hope, by the answers given, we turn now to consider the main ethical problem. Following the considerations of Chapter I, we could give it no other form than, "Why does man act morally? (or, "Why *is* he moral?" But this comes to the same thing, for in the end his character can be known only through his conduct). Since, in two earlier chapters, we attempted to answer the questions "What are the motives of human conduct?" and "What is the meaning of moral?" it appears that we need only unite the results there found to have the solution of our problem at hand.

This shall, in fact, be our procedure. But in carrying it out we see that we touch on all of the points which, in discussions of moral matters, constitute the most important topics of dispute. In order to be able to decide this dispute we have, in the remaining chapters, analyzed certain questions whose answers are presupposed by many of the following considerations. In such considerations we come upon questions which are not only the most important human questions, but which are the *only* important questions. For only those things are important which relate to values, and it lies in the nature of the problems of value that all without exception are affected in some way by the main problem of ethics. Of course this is not the place in which to decide practical moral problems, but we shall at least have to establish general principles with whose help such decisions may be facilitated, wherever it is possible.

The answer to the question of what in general is the motive of human conduct ran: in the case of conscious volitional conduct (ethics is not interested in other activities) men are always determined by *feelings,* and in such a manner that they always strive for that goal, among those considered, the idea of which is characterized, at the time of choice, by the least pain or the greatest pleasure (the nature of this comparison of magnitudes has been carefully elucidated).

And the answer to the question, "What is the meaning of moral?" was, "That conduct which society believes will best further its own welfare."

If we put the two results together we see that the main problem, "Why do men act morally?" will be solved as soon as we can show how the idea of the things which appear useful to society can also be pleasant for the individual agent himself. Moreover, the explanation must make clear why this is not always so, for there are also cases of immoral conduct.

First, we must take care to understand what is meant by "explanation" in this context. In many cases it is certainly quite impossible to give a psychological explanation of why a definite experience is pleasant.

Thus it is an ultimate, irreducible fact that a sweet taste-sensation is generally pleasant, while, on the contrary, a very bitter or sour one is unpleasant; and the same holds of the feeling components of every sensuous experience. There are at best but physiological or biological explanations for the joy we experience in a saturated color, in the sexual act, in the satisfaction of thirst, and so forth; and these do not interest the philosopher. These facts have never been considered as problematic. The philosophers have never asked, "Why does it please men to eat, to dance, to rest?" They asked only, "How can it please men to do what pleases *others*?"

Therefore there are two classes of joys: those which we take as natural, elementary, not in need of any explanation; and those which do not seem to be self-evident, but excite philosophic wonder. To this latter class aesthetics and ethics owe their existence. Their task is to explain why feelings of pleasure (or pain) occur also where, at first, we do not expect them (with what reason, though?). The joys of the second sort can, evidently, be explained only because they can be referred to those of the first kind. Knowledge always consists only in such a reduction of what is to be explained to something not requiring explanation. Thus it must be shown how the aesthetic and ethical joys and valuations are derived from or compounded of "natural" or "primitive" feelings of pleasure. We shall speak later of the psychological laws which govern the "combination" of feelings. At present the following

problem faces us: what are the primitive feeling reactions which may be considered so natural that an
explanation of all the remaining ones, which refer to
them, will satisfy us as a complete explanation?

1. *What Are the "Natural" Impulses?*

Most philosophers have been altogether too naïve
in their assumptions regarding what they considered
to be primitive human nature.   They are most to blame
if they failed to see the problem, and thus failed to
indicate by *what means* they actually wished to make
their explanation—proceeding as they did from some
confused idea of man as a naturally egoistic creature.
How confused such an idea is was shown in Chapter
III.   The for the most part obscurely expressed fundamental idea was, perhaps, that the natural impulses
are those which are absolutely necessary for mere biological existence, hence those directed upon ingestion,
warmth, and reproduction.   Thus other men are considered only as so many obstacles to the satisfaction
of one's own impulses; for other men, too, claim the
things needed for existence.   And because men quar-
rel mutually over these things there arises the "war
of all against all," which Hobbes assumed to be the
primitive state, since he, in fact, began with the described presuppositions.   Now it is undoubtedly true
and interesting that, beginning with these assumptions, one can deduce the necessity of ending the *bel-
lum omnium contra omnes* by, as it were, a peace, and

reaching a *modus vivendi* in which each leaves to the others a part of the world's goods, in order thus to enjoy his own share in safety. As we see, in this manner one easily gains the insight that for a human being of such nature it would be best (and indeed the best thing for the preservation of his life) if each one observed such rules of conduct, approximately, as are actually established by the legislation of a state.

But the question of what would be the best for a man is to be sharply distinguished from the other question, of why he actually does what is best. In order to answer it, following this line of thought, we must now make an assumption regarding the individual's *intelligence*. If everyone possessed the keen understanding of Hobbes, and knew how to use it in making his decisions, then under certain conditions a sufficiently strong motive could be formed for the discovery of and obedience to such a rule of behavior: the idea of the personal joy to be obtained by obeying the law would constitute such a motive, because of a transference of its pleasure-tone to the idea of the means leading to this end. But since in fact the intellectual capacities are not so great, and since mere intellectual operations have very little influence on the feelings, the motive of proper conduct is not the result of such a calculation. Additional motives must be supplied, and society introduces sanctions, that is, threatens transgression of the rules with artificial punishment. And now the motive does not consist in the joy of the foreseen natural consequences of the act, but in the fear of the consequences of wrong conduct, that is, fear of pain. In this fear lies the beginning of what is called *conscience;* of its further development, whereby it becomes relatively independent of external sanctions, one can, to a certain extent, also give a psychological explanation.

But this whole chain of reasoning has little value, because it begins with a fictional human nature which quite definitely does not correspond to reality. The most important ties that naturally bind men to their environment are here left out of account. Just as one cannot think of man's nature apart from his breathing, which joins him with the external world, so we cannot consider his nature independently of the human atmosphere in which he lives from his birth on. In other words: the *social* impulses, by virtue of which the behavior of others constitutes an *immediate* source of pleasure and pain for him, are just as "natural" as the most primitive bodily needs; and are not derived from them in some roundabout way. If such genesis of the social impulses must be assumed anywhere, it has long since been completed on prehuman evolutionary levels; these impulses are present in some form or other in all higher animals. The need for companionship is found very widespread in the herd instinct, and the same holds of those instincts which aid in the rearing of the young; and hundreds of similar examples are generally known. Ought the philosopher to search for their genesis, and meddle in biology? He will certainly not desire to undertake this task: his

interests lie in another direction, and he must formulate his questions so that they may be answered by
an investigation of the human soul alone.

2. *New Formulation of the Question*

But, if Hobbes' fiction is not acceptable, what other
point of departure shall we accept? What then are
the "natural" human dispositions? Which of man's
possible ends-in-view can we assume to be naturally
pleasant, and not surprising and in need of explanation? Shall we add to hunger, thirst, and the sexual
impulse, say, the mother instinct, and the impulse toward companionship, and four or five other inclinations, and then on this new basis begin Hobbes' whole
deduction anew? In this manner the philosopher
would win himself no great merit. Of course, with
the help of the social impulses it would be easier for
him to explain the observance of laws, and the moral
behavior proceeding from this, than it would be upon
the basis of the Hobbesian presuppositions. He would
be able to ascribe to the altruistic inclinations a part in
the stirrings of "conscience," and would stay closer to
the facts in his considerations. But his explanation
would never be able to do full justice to the facts, for
the selection of impulses which he assumes to be
"natural" would always remain arbitrary. It would
always be a matter for doubt whether other equally
primitive dispositions were not to be added, or whether,
on the contrary, the number assumed could not be

reduced. But as long as this is the case, the whole deduction loses its peculiar interest: if one may suppose the most diverse social inclinations to be proper to human nature, then moral conduct in general ceases to be surprising. One is convinced in principle that morality is in complete conformity with human nature, and it becomes a question of secondary importance as to which impulses in particular must be adduced to give an account of why men actually do what society demands of them.

This whole explanatory procedure is unsatisfying because it fails to emphasize what, at bottom, most interests the philosopher, namely, the *differences* in human behavior. He desires to explain morality, and therefore must assume men to be creatures endowed with definite dispositions. The interest not only of the moralists, but also of the psychologists, is centered, primarily, upon the question: Why does this man have feelings in conformity with moral laws, while that man does not? Why is one man good, the other bad? What does the one have which the other lacks? And to this is joined the practical problem of how he can be supplied with what he lacks.

In these questions we are not at all helped by the distinction between natural and derived impulses. We shall not wish to asume that the "bad" man is natural, and that the "good" man has, in addition to the primitive dispositions, certain others developed from them; we shall, rather, accept every inclination which we find in men as belonging to human nature, excluding only those which are notoriously morbid, and generally recognized as such (in which we need not draw the boundaries too sharply, and in any case we shall include the characteristic of *rarity* in the criterion of morbidity). And now our task would be to explain moral and immoral decisions in particular cases, or rather in *typical cases,* by indicating which of the available stock of impulses have actually been functioning as motives.

The solution of the problem thus formulated would be extremely difficult. It would require an understanding of the realm of impulses and their nuances and demand an insight into the laws of emotional life which we do not possess. And even if we did possess such knowledge its application would meet with the greatest difficulties because of its extreme complexity. Therefore it is necessary to simplify the problem further, so that we may ignore the concrete obstacles and speak only of those general principles necessary for the solution of the problem.

To this end we turn our attention to a further circumstance, which our considerations have neglected hitherto. We have viewed man's inclinations as fixed constituents of his nature or character, but it is their essential property to be, to a considerable degree, *changeable.* The impulses do not form a solid framework of the soul, but constitute rather a plastic mass, which, under the influence of the environment, is constantly changing. The philosopher has a much greater interest in these changes than in individual

differences of conduct and character. The question
of their origin and disappearance is more important
than that of their differences, and by the transformation of these inclinations those differences can be created or destroyed; or, to put it crudely, a better man
can be made of a bad one. Although the impulses
are of many forms and their connections very complicated, there is, following from their nature, a simple
law governing their changes, to which all of them are
subject. Hence, what is most important in them for
us is open to knowledge; without its being necessary
for one to fall into the difficulties which, because of
the complexity of the psychic life, grow out of a strict
explanation of human decisions. If, in this manner,
we pay less attention to the dispositions themselves
than to the laws governing their changes, we introduce
a differential calculus, as it were, instead of the usual
one; and the form of the question must be altered.
Therefore we renounce the attempt to give an explicit
answer to the question of why men are moral. And
we do this with no regret, because everything important
concerning it is implicitly answered by the reply to the
question which we now ask: by what means are human
dispositions toward moral behavior increased or de-
creased?

This form of the question will forthwith undergo a
further change, and then take, approximately, the form
which we have already given it in the chapter heading.
For the present we see, at least, why the main question
(the answer to which constitutes, according to the con-

siderations of Chapter I, the ultimate goal of all ethical inquiry) could not appear in the present chapter heading.

3. Moral Suggestion

The influences which affect a man's inclinations for a change, favorably or unfavorably, can be grouped, roughly, into those which influence him from without, and those which result from his own conduct. The division is not precise, for the external world is usually more or less involved in influences of the second sort; but it serves our present purpose.

We need devote only a brief discussion to the factors of the first sort, as being less important to ethics. In doing so we exclude purely physical or physiological factors, because they do not enter into this context (even though the opinion has been expressed that future science will control human character merely by the infusion of certain hormones), and restrict ourselves to those of psychology. Here we come upon *suggestion*, which plays a role from childhood up in the formation of desires and inclinations, the importance of which can hardly be overestimated. A thing can become the goal of desire if, without giving any reasons, it is but constantly praised. If we always hear that a thing is good, even though it is not stated why or for what it is good, the idea of that thing becomes pleasant; we desire to make its acquaintance or to possess it. If we see many desiring the same thing, if, say, we observe how an irresistible current draws individuals and nations to the south or the west a similar desire awakens in us. The best-known example of the process of making the idea of an object pleasant by means of suggestion, and thus making the object itself into a goal of desire, is the advertisement. In order to achieve its astonishing effect it needs, often, only to associate the name of the object with an attractive picture; the pleasure in the picture alone has the consequence that the beholder likes to think of the object; it becomes *valuable* to him. Of course, if, in addition, it does not possess some utility, the purchaser will be deceived, and will reject the advertisement as misleading. But because of the difficulty, frequently, of determining its utility value, suggestion often remains the only source of the pleasure which the object is able to produce.

What is the case with morality? Its precepts, too, can be made valuable by praise; for the method of suggestion is, in principle, applicable to *every* object. And in fact this means is used to create motives for moral conduct; the educator presents moral behavior to the child as the most excellent of all goals, he takes every opportunity of extolling the grandeur of noble deeds, of recommending noble persons as patterns that cannot be lauded too highly. Certainly in such a manner joy is aroused in good deeds and in good men, and the desire is created of emulating them. Here there is, of course, at once added a second motive, difficult to separate from the first: if good deeds are really universally praised and the doer of them enjoys the respect of his fellow men, then the obedient pupil will share in this welcome consequence of good behavior; and thus new motives are added. To be sure, experience can teach him later that noble conduct is often misinterpreted, and earns him persecution instead of honor and recognition. And this would work against the pleasure induced by suggestion, as in the case of a cheap article greatly praised in advertisement, if the suggestion is not so formulated as to run no risk from this quarter. As a matter of fact the good educator does not speak of external results; he lauds decisions which are made independently of another person's knowledge, and says that the good which is done secretly is especially praiseworthy. In this manner the emphasis upon the pleasure produced by suggestion is separated from other motives. Of course an unpleasant motive can be created in the same way: the expression of universal disgust for a definite mode of behavior makes the idea of it unpleasant also, even though no reason for the disgust be given.

This process of forming motives by suggestion is thoroughly effective, and there are no objections to it. Or might it be condemned "from the moral standpoint"? Clearly only if the value of a thing lay entirely in the fact that it was universally praised; in which case it would not seem to us to be genuine, but only, as it were, a soap bubble, which would collapse at the first impact. It would be a piece of worthless paper which passed from hand to hand in a closed envelope and was acknowledged as payment by everyone because each believed that a check lay within—until someone opened the envelope and cried "Fraud!"

One renders no great service to morality by wishing to brand the opening of the envelope itself as immoral conduct, that is, to ban the question, "Why in the world should morality be praised?" (which Kant and the champions of absolute value theories are inclined to do). Thus Nietzsche might come along and say: behold, I have been the first to unveil so-called morality, and what did I find? Merely that the traditional precepts have indeed a real value, but only for those who impose them upon others and who do not themselves obey; for these others the precepts have only the value induced by suggestion, by which the masters delude them, and otherwise none at all.

Still, it might be possible that society, which, as we saw, is the originator of moral precepts, resembles a dishonest merchant who praises worthless goods for his own ends. If this were so, then of course my moral behavior would bring joy to *others* (the society which commands is always composed of the others. I cannot count myself of their number), but for me my behavior would have only an apparent value which the others were clever enough to suggest to me. But such is not in the least the case. And should an individual once doubt this and, untroubled by moral commands, give free rein to his impulses, society would at once react with the imposition of sanctions, and would, by punishment, show him a true value of morality, consisting simply in avoiding these sanctions.

And thus we would arrive at the other external factors which, in addition to suggestion, influence human inclinations: namely, punishment and reward, which see to it that in fact feelings of pleasure are the result of following desired modes of conduct, and that pain is the consequence of forbidden conduct. The ideas of such results are then stressed correspondingly and function as motives.

But these matters have already been touched upon several times, and are familiar to every child. Consideration of these external factors in the formation and repression of dispositions leads only to insight into relatively external processes, and makes intelligible only the roughest outlines of conduct, as we noticed previously. Suggestion and reference to social sanctions are of course only the most primitive means of the production of motive feelings; the *subtle* influences which most interest the philosopher are not to be attained by their help. We already know that the social impulses themselves contribute stronger and more permanent motives.

Hence it is time to turn to those character-forming influences which come from within and are established by one's own acts.

4. *Motive Feelings and Realization Feelings*

All volitional conduct comes to pass in this manner: one of several different conflicting ends-in-view finally gains the foreground of consciousness and represses

the others; this, of course, occurs as soon as the positive
difference between its feeling-tone and those of the
others passes beyond a certain point, so that the most
pleasant or least painful idea emerges victoriously.
The feeling connected with the idea (that is, with the
so-called end-in-view), in particular the feeling joined
to the victorious idea, we called the motive feeling.
And it was one of our most important observations
that the feeling which the idea of a definite state
awakens in us need not be at all similar to the feeling
which belongs to the state itself when it is realized.
We shall call the latter the realization feeling. A realization pleasure as well as a realization pain can thus
correspond to a motive pleasure, and vice versa. We
must, as we stated earlier, distinguish sharply between
the idea of a pleasant state and the pleasant idea of a
state.

Hence an unpleasant effect can be imagined with
pleasure, that is, can be desired and willed. It is this
fact to which one can rightly point in order to refute
the thesis, carelessly formulated by hedonism, that men
can seek nothing but "happiness." For happiness consists always of pleasant states. It is not the case that
a *de facto* unpleasant state can be a goal only so long
as its true feeling components are not known; but a
man can very well *know* that he is proceeding toward
unhappiness and still do so.

In spite of this, in the thesis of the exclusive striving
for happiness there lies, deep within, a kernel of truth;
and I deliberately described it as carelessly "formu-

lated." It is not merely the fact that all volition is
determined just by the excess of pleasure in the motive
experienced by him who wills, although this is important enough; for this fact signifies that, in the last
analysis, it is always only a matter of the feelings of
the agent; that there is no possibility of influencing
him in any other way than by arousing his own feelings; that, above all, there is no bridge from man to
man which does not first lead over individual feelings.
Here lies the source of the final, awful loneliness of
man, from which there is no escape, because each individual, each consciousness is enclosed within itself;
so that its feelings can be only its own feelings and
can never be felt also by another. The social impulses,
too, but institute a mutual dependence among the
feelings of different individuals; they cannot make
these feelings identical, and one tries in vain by means
of a metaphysic of "universal will" or "super-individual
spirit" to conjure away the difficulty.

It is, I say, not alone this fact of the exclusive determination of the will of each individual by his own
pleasure which constitutes the real essence of the proposition expressing the universal striving for happiness,
but a different fact, the consideration of which will
now lead us to the most important regularity which
underlies the transformation of impulses by conduct.
I refer to the fact that there is a certain dependence
between the motive pleasure and the realization pleasure
or pain, even though this is not so simple as hedonism
assumed: namely, that the motive feeling and the real-

ization feeling must either be both pleasant or both painful; that therefore, for example, the idea of a pleasant end must necessarily be a pleasant idea of the end. Experience teaches us that this is not always so, and often not even when the person who wills is perfectly aware of the pain joined to the state for which he strives. However, two things may be said here in order to mitigate the importance of the facts which argue against the happiness thesis.

First, one could say that the states thus striven for are, at best, of the "suffering" variety whose mixed character we have expressly indicated, and that their pleasure components had, perhaps, something to do with the possibility of such motivation. I believe that there is some truth in this argument, that, thus, the representation of a purely repulsive, hopeless condition may not be pleasant; and that in the suffering which a resigned person takes upon himself there is always also represented a state of satisfaction in the consummated act; but this would alter nothing in the fact that suffering is chosen in preference to other, pleasant situations.

And, secondly, one might think that the idea of an unpleasant end could be pleasant only in so far as it did not picture the end itself exactly, and left out essential or other features. If one should picture the end to oneself with perfect liveliness, as it in fact will be when realized, and neither obliterate nor palliate anything in the idea, then it must certainly exhibit the same feeling components as the end itself would, were it realized. In this argument, too, there may be some truth; but since the agreement between the idea and what the idea represents can never be perfect, and since we must deal with psychic processes as they actually take place, we cannot make this argument basic.

5. *The Assimilation of Motive Feelings to Realization Feelings*

Now it seems to me that behind these objections there lies a real point, namely: the discrepancy between the motive feeling and the realization feeling, even though it cannot be denied, still represents a situation which cannot endure. That is, whenever such a discrepancy between the feelings occurs, forces are at once set to work to equalize them. By means of the natural process which leads from motives through conduct to realization and then to new motives and conduct, the impulses (which are the dispositions to have definite feelings in the presence of definite ideas) are transformed, so that the motive feeling and realization feeling come into agreement with one another.

The mechanism according to which this takes place is easy to understand. If a goal that is thought of with pleasure is actually attained and arouses strong feelings of pain in the agent, then the pain will, in the future, associate itself with the newly formed ideas of one's goal, and will work against the pleasure tone which it formerly had. Upon repetition this tendency will increase, and so on until the goal no longer can be desired, because at last to the pain of the realization there corresponds a painful motive. If, conversely, a condition at first shunned is realized once or often against the wishes of the individual, so that the joy which actually lies within it is experienced by him, it will inevitably come to pass that the idea of that state slowly (or even suddenly) becomes pleasant, and that thus an inclination arises to renew it. And further, if a situation that hitherto had been always pleasant in its realization somehow ceases to be so, for example, because of a physiological process ("satiety" and so forth) then the pain now experienced in it will presently be transmitted to the idea of the situation; and the impulse directed upon it disappears. This is all nothing but the usual process of "experience," and one can easily find hundreds of examples of it in daily life. It is obvious that this process, as is the case with every natural process, can be cut across by others with an opposite effect; thus insane ideas or constant and systematic obstacles can hinder the accommodation of motive feelings to realization feelings in special cases. We take cognizance of this in saying only that there is a *tendency* toward assimilation of that discrepancy. But this tendency is in the long run insurmountable; and, since we assert its existence, we have actually formulated a general rule which governs the whole emotional life, and which can serve us as a guide in the solution of our problem.

6. *The Foundation of Hedonism*

What follows from the principle of the assimilation of motive feelings to realization feelings?

First, that a complex of dispositions in which these disagree cannot be stable, but bears within itself the tendency toward change as experience progresses. If we wish to generate lasting dependable dispositions in a person, we must take care that the realization pleasure contains what the motive pleasure promises. In other words: the principle of assimilation makes it impossible to prescribe a definite mode of behavior permanently to a man if obedience to the rule brings him only an increase in pain. Expressed still otherwise: the motive pleasure can be permanently kindled only by realization pleasure; in all other attempts to nourish it, it is finally extinguished. Of course, fixed (innate) impulses can be so powerful in the case of a definitely formed physiological constitution that the principle of assimilation remains powerless against them, at least during the individual's lifetime; and then we ascribe a "morbid" strength to them. But such inclinations as we produce in men (by means of education in its widest sense) have no prospect of survival if the principle works against them. Only those desires are stable, only those inclinations guarantee harmony which are directed toward truly pleasant ends, or, if one prefers, toward *happiness*. This seems to me to be the truth which underlies the assertion that man can strive only for happiness.

If to the motive pleasure there corresponds a pure realization pain, then the individual feels himself somehow deceived, even if he knew beforehand that the result would cause him suffering. He feels himself betrayed by his desires. We can now say that there is only *one* way to create motives of conduct which will prevail against all influences; and this is by *reference to actual happy consequences*.

This is, of course, an ancient truth. We know that it expresses nothing more than the principle upon which rests punishment and reward and the procedure of sanctions in the state, in religion, and in daily life. And of course, when we claim the way of sanctions as the only ultimate one in the case of *moral* behavior also, this seems to be a very uninspiring attitude, upon which recent ethics looks down with contempt. Such contempt is perhaps justified in reference to the extremely primitive *argument* with which hedonism and eudaemonism are accustomed to defend their position; but the above derivation has nothing in common with such arguments, and neither do the traditional hedonistic formulations coincide with our thesis, which says only that invincible motives for obeying moral rules exist only when pleasure follows upon such obedience.

If we review for a moment, we see that we have now provisionally answered the question, "How are human dispositions toward moral behavior strengthened or weakened?" in such a manner that we say: the dispo-

sitions toward moral conduct in a man can, indeed, be
strengthened by external means, such as suggestion
and artificial punishment and rewards; but the inclinations thus created must be transient and be wiped
out, inevitably, by the process of assimilation *if moral
conduct is not itself a source of pleasure, or does not
disclose such sources.* But if it does, then the motives,
whatever be their origin, will be strengthened and
made firm by this same process; and they will have
the tendency to become permanent impulses.

Therefore, in order to know the laws that govern
the origin of inclinations toward moral behavior, it is
necessary, above all, to investigate the pleasure value
of such behavior itself. Everything depends upon
whether it is valuable for the agent himself, that is,
whether it is productive of pleasure. For if this be
not the case the fairest motives run the danger of losing
all their power. And they *must* finally lose it (perhaps only in the course of generations). If we imagine
the associational assimilative process, whereby this occurs, transported into the light of reflective consciousness, we can say: a moment arrives at which a man
finds no satisfactory answer to the question: why in
the world should I act in this manner? other than:
because it brings me happiness! It follows from the
universally valid law of volition that he can will only
such ends as are valuable for him. However, he will
then distinguish genuine from spurious values: both
are real, but the latter can be destroyed by the assimilative process. Spurious values exist by virtue of the

pleasure which belongs to the *idea* of the end alone, and not to the end itself; while genuine values consist in those feelings of pleasure with which the end itself is experienced.

Thus we are confronted by the question: are the ends commended to us in the moral precepts really genuine values for the individual, or do they consist in the feelings of pleasure with which society has been clever enough to equip the ideas of the ends desired by itself?   We are confronted by the ancient problem: does virtue lead to happiness?

Should the answer chance to be in the affirmative we should certainly be quite satisfied, and should believe ourselves to have solved the fundamental ethical problem in so far as this can be done by means of general considerations.   But if, as many philosophers suppose, a negative answer must be given, we should still like to know (running the risk that those philosophers will consider such a question unworthy) what does lead to happiness, if not virtue?   And, hence, we finally reach the question that constitutes our present chapter heading.   We seek the path that leads to value; after finding it we shall see whether it is the same as the path of moral conduct or not.

7. *Happiness and the Capacity for Happiness*

In these final considerations we have several times used the word "happiness" somewhat carelessly, though we are aware of the considerable vagueness in its meaning, which renders it unfit for the expression of precise thoughts. We have, evidently, used it as simply synonymous with pleasant states; but much more lies in the meaning of the word, namely, a superlative. By it we wish to designate not just any pleasant state, but those of maximum pleasure, the most joyful experiences. Indeed, many would hesitate to use the word at all for individual states, and would say that a life through which were spread many moderate joys contained more happiness than one which consisted of a few moments of the highest bliss, separated by long intervals of great pain. The essential immeasureability and incomparability of feelings, which we touched upon in Chapters II and IV, seem to make comparisons of happiness senseless and the word itself meaningless; but still there must, obviously, be some sense in which to make such distinctions in an individual's life, for they do play an important practical role. And for our purposes, too, these distinctions are indispensable; for it would not in the least suffice to find the path to just anything valuable: we must rather seek the path to what is *most* valuable. If any more definite meaning can be found for this superlative, nothing would stand in the way of designating it by the word "happiness." For he who has seen, with us, that values are to be founded only upon feelings of pleasure will at once identify the concept of happiness with that of the most valuable.

Hence it must be possible to find some substitute for the meaningless summation or addition of experiences of pleasure, by means of which they can somehow be compared and put into an order. We succeeded in finding a substitute in certain psychic processes for the pleasure factors which strive with one another in the motivation of volitional conduct (p. 40). However, here where we are not concerned with adjacent motivating feelings but with realization values, the difficulty is greater. I can offer no universally valid substitute; but perhaps it will suffice to point out a very important one, which fits definite cases, and which may possibly be generalized. If we think of two joys of which the one after enjoyment leaves a man essentially unchanged, while the gratification of the other makes a repetition of it or the enjoyment of another either difficult or impossible, then we shall be able to say of the second that, in all probability, it makes life less rich in pleasure, even if considered in itself it should be very great. Hence, we shall ascribe a much greater "happiness-value" to the first. (As an example of the second kind we may mention the use of poisonous intoxicants, or intense sensual pleasures which have a stupefying effect, and so forth.) Thus we have here the possibility of speaking of the contribution of a particular joy to the "total pleasure," or of its effect upon the "totality of happiness," without having to perform any addition, and without thinking of the concept of the total sum itself. And we make use of this possibility by considering the effect of the gratification of impulses upon the capacity of men for future feelings of pleasure; in short, upon their *capacity for happiness*. And therefore we take a step forward. For if we shall not be able to indicate more exactly the way leading to what is most valuable (and we certainly shall not be able to do so) we shall have pointed out, at least, a very important sign-post if we say it would in any case lead through such modes of behavior as least reduce the capacity for happiness, or perhaps even increase it. The capacity for feelings of pleasure is a property of the human constitution, and as such may be difficult to conceive, but it is still infinitely more easily comprehended than the nebulous, ever-elusive concept of happiness itself.

8. *The Happiness Value of Social Impulses*

With the means now at our disposal, even though they are meagre enough, we can begin to advance toward the solution of our problem. If the mode of behavior leading to the most valuable life is that which procures for a man the greatest joys, along with the least restrictions on his capacity for happiness, then the immediate question is: what are the inclinations from which such behavior proceeds?

More penetrating investigations than these can be must examine the various sorts of human impulses with respect to their power for bringing happiness; we rest satisfied with pointing out the most impressive facts which especially distinguish individual groups of motives. Here experience teaches us something which, strangely, is viewed by most people as very surprising, and so paradoxical that they do not believe it at all, and actually are of the opinion that experience teaches us just the contrary; while it is in fact anything but wonderful. I have no doubt that experience indicates very clearly that the *social* impulses are those which best assure their bearers of a joyful life.

The social impulses are those dispositions of a person by virtue of which the idea of a pleasant or unpleasant state of *another* person is itself a pleasant or unpleasant experience (also the mere perception of another creature, his presence alone, can, by virtue of such an impulse, elicit feelings of pleasure). The natural effect of these inclinations is that their bearer establishes the joyful states of others as ends of his conduct. And upon realization of these ends he enjoys the resultant pleasure; for not only the idea, but also the actual perception of the expression of joy pleases him. Hence there is a *genuine* value, for there is an agreement of the motive feeling and the realization feeling.

The reason that the happiness value of social inclinations seems *a priori* incredible to many philosophers lies clearly in the fact that these impulses are directed toward *another's* welfare; and must not the impulses which bring happiness to their bearer be directed, rather, toward his own welfare? This view so widely held is in truth extremely shortsighted, and at its roots lie all of those misunderstandings which stand in the way of the insight into the facts described in Chapters II and III. There simply is no impulse directed toward "personal welfare," and there can be none; for the very concept contains a sort of vicious circle. "Personal welfare," that is, one's own satisfaction, consists just in the gratification of impulses—an impulse directed toward the satisfaction of all impulses is obviously nonsense. In itself (that is, apart from consequences) what an impulse is directed toward is quite indifferent to the resultant joy, and there is not the least essential reason why, for example, the pleasure in filling one's stomach should be in any way distinguished from the joy one has upon looking into eyes shining with happiness. The latter joy may be more difficult to understand in biological-genetic terms, but this, above all, concerns neither the philosopher nor the psychologist.

If I may consider this last example, the coarseness of which be forgiven, the above-mentioned criterion of the conservation of the capacity for happiness can be illustrated. The satisfaction of hunger as the condition of existence is of course also a presupposition of future joys. But it is common knowledge that the satisfaction of the impulse of nourishment is "salutary" only within definite limits; an excess can so alter the whole constitution that one's entire life becomes poorer, in that (even apart from direct illness) the ability to enjoy the highest pleasures is itself stifled by excessive gratification of the palate. And the same seems to hold of all impulses which correspond to immediate "bodily" needs: unrestrained gratification of these impulses diminishes the realization pleasure; and processes which dull the senses and result in enervation lead to a reaction in the organism which diminishes its capacity for happiness. Such impulses are indeed very necessary, but their happiness value is relatively small. Physiologically there corresponds to them a robust but coarse mechanism which is set in motion by strong sensory stimuli, but which fails to penetrate the higher centers, where the correlate of complicated, delicate "higher" inclinations is to be sought. Their satisfaction reacts quite differently upon the organism, making it ever more differentiated and more susceptible to new joys, indeed more sensitive on the whole.

Thus we meet with the distinction and opposition of the "lower" and "higher" pleasures, which is really fundamental for the conduct of life, and has rightly played the greatest role in the wisdom of all ages. To be sure, it has often been misunderstood, as if it dealt with a primary distinction between "good" and "bad" pleasures; and has increased the prejudice against "pleasure" and aided the theories of absolute value, which we saw to be so pernicious to ethics. Its true nature, however, is to be found only in the facts just described.

Now the social impulses, too, belong to the "finer," "higher" group of impulses which presuppose a more complicated psychic life. No one will suppose that these impulses can have a "pernicious" effect upon the psychic constitution of their bearers; but the positive influence their application and satisfaction exercise upon the differentiation of the soul, which thereby becomes susceptible of ever finer moods, is too little emphasized. Even friendly association with *animals* clearly has this effect. We must add, also, the external happy consequences. The social impulses constitute a truly ingenious means of multiplying the feelings of pleasure; for the man who feels the pleasures of his fellow men to be a source of his own pleasure thereby increases his joys with the increase in theirs, he shares their happiness; while the egoist is, so to speak, restricted to his own pleasure. The objection that social feelings have as a consequence the sharing of sorrow is partly justified, but does not weigh so heavily, because suffering too gives scope to the satisfaction of the social impulses, in that one can work for its alleviation. Further, there belong to the external happy consequences those of which one is, perhaps, first inclined to think; namely, the reactions produced in the objects of the social impulses. In part the bearer of such impulses himself will be chosen as a preferred object of the social impulses of others; and in part society guarantees him, as a very useful member, all possible advantages.

Pessimists like to point to instances where such "natural reward" of social behavior fails to be made, and the benefactor reaps ingratitude and envy, or is ridiculed and abused. It is true that under such unfavorable circumstances pain can be added to the pleasant result which is always connected with the satisfaction of social impulses; pain which sometimes even annuls the pleasure, and thus counteracts and finally overcomes the motive pleasure (embitterment). But these are really unusual circumstances, and it is cer-

tainly unnecessary to take them into consideration in
the description of the normal working out of social
impulses. Experience on the average (there is in these
matters only an average experience) does not confirm
pessimism. For this reason at the very beginning of
this discussion I advisedly pointed to *experience* as fur-
nishing the proof that the social impulses increase the
capacity for happiness; and this makes the deductive
derivation unnecessary.

However, the clearest hint that experience offers us
in this respect is the fact that the highest feelings of
happiness ever known to us are due to a social impulse:
namely, *love*. No one has yet succeeded in making at
all intelligible why it is that the greatest bliss is joined
to this most perfect of social impulses, and it has been
attempted but very rarely. Was the discouragement
due perhaps to the magnitude of the task? In any
case the explanation does not lie in the inner union
with bodily needs, which we have in the case of sexual
love. For, however important this connection be (it
proves, as it were, the nobility and equal rank of the
sensual pleasures) yet these things are separable, and
are often really separated. And thus we see that mu-
tuality, that is, the social motive, plays the chief role,
and not the specific contact, the bodily motive. Therefore we may take the most exalted fact of all experience
as an indication that those inclinations which are
directed upon the joys of others bear the greatest possibilities of happiness.

It is not necessary for our general purpose to consider the different varieties and nuances of social impulses; but so much may be mentioned: the description here given applies to the inclinations which relate individual to individual rather than to the more diffuse impulses of "universal love of mankind," "feelings of solidarity," "love of one's own nation," and so forth. These, for the most part, deserve to be viewed with a certain distrust; for often with them the concern is with a very pleasing idea, cherished and protected in the mind, rather than with the actual happiness of others. An impulse which, for example, directs itself upon the "greatest happiness of the greatest number," as utilitarianism must demand in order to realize its moral principle, seems to me to be an absurdity. Genuine sympathy can develop only on the basis of definite qualities of the beloved: it does not require any adaptation of others to one's own way of thinking (which intolerant demand is characteristic of many forms of "universal love of mankind").

9. *Virtue and Happiness*

The form in which the social impulses express themselves is *good conduct,* or altruism. This opposition to egoism is one of the most essential marks of *moral* behavior. Hence, in any case, the most important motives of morality are found in the altruistic impulses, and many have thought *the only ones;* thus, for example, with Schopenhauer, who wished to derive every moral disposition from *sympathy,* and with many Eng-

lish moral philosophers who declared sympathy to be
the source of all virtues. However this may be, if
these same dispositions which lead to the greatest possibilities of pleasure are identical with those from which,
for the most part, virtuous conduct springs, this means
that virtue and happiness have the same causes, that
they must go hand in hand.

I am firmly convinced that experience clearly demonstrates this dependence. I have never been able
to conceive how this can be denied, and am always
astonished at the superficiality of the observations and
arguments by which men seek to prove that happiness
and morality have nothing to do with one another;
indeed to prove that virtue is detrimental to felicity,
and that a robust egoism must be recommended to him
who seeks happiness. What is usually said in confirmation of this opinion? Well, one points out that
the rich and powerful, and all those who "prosper,"
do not usually tend to be the best, and cites some poet-
ical words describing how the scoundrel drives along
"in a golden coach," while the good man stands by
the wayside bowed down with misery.

Two points should be noted regarding this argument.
In the first place, these philosophers for whom virtue
and bliss cannot be separated far enough still presuppose for the sake of the argument a concept of "happiness" which they would never seriously accept in practice, and with which they can do far less than justice
to human nature. Consider what Kant himself in his
argumentation pictured as the earthly gifts of fortune!

No, the majority of men know very well that wealth, for example, is of no very great value, and much prefer to be surrounded by love, to have well-bred children, and so forth; and the philosopher will not readily admit that the "scoundrel" has any prospect of sharing in such goods.

And secondly, the described opposing arguments quite misunderstand the true meaning of the statements regarding the happiness value of virtue. The fate of a man depends to a great extent upon circumstances which are quite independent of his conduct, for example, upon "chance," upon the path taken by a bullet, or by a tiny bacillus; and only a fool could believe that virtue is a means of avoiding the great misfortunes to which life is, to such a degree, subject. Our statement, therefore, obviously cannot assert (as many Stoics sought to assert) that virtue *guarantees* a joyful life, but only that it leads to the greatest happiness possible *under the given external conditions* of life; and it can of course assert this only with probability. For an accident can always put an end to everything; as it can suddenly change everthing for the better—hence it is clear that no rule of life, no general proposition concerning the effect of any behavior can take it into account. The blows of fate cannot be influenced, and have nothing to do with morality; but what our *mood* is under given external conditions, and what kind of influence the blows have upon us, does depend upon our impulses and behavior. The virtuous man and the scoundrel are equally subject to chance, the sun shines upon the good and the evil; and therefore the assertion regarding the relation between virtue and happiness says only that the good man always has better *prospects* of the most joyful life than does the egoist, that the former enjoys a greater *capacity* for happiness than does the latter.

If the virtuous man has better prospects, that is, a greater probability of joy, then, on the average, good men must be happier than egoists. And experience so clearly confirms this that it must be visible to every open eye. Is not the good man also the more cheerful? Does not the eye of one who looks with love upon his fellow men shine with a joy which we seek in vain in the cold glance of the egoist? Here again we are furnished with a very remarkable indication of the truth of what we are saying. For, if we apply to the *smile* the approved method of studying affects in the form of their externalizations, which served us earlier in our consideration of tears, we see that the same delightful play of facial muscles is at once the expression of both joy and kindness. Man smiles when he is gay, and also when he feels sympathy; kindness and happiness have the same facial expression; the friendly man is also the happy man, and vice versa. I believe that there is no clearer indication of the inner relationship of happiness and a noble disposition than that which nature itself offers.

The happiness of love and the phenomenon of the smile seem to me to be the two important facts upon which ethics can base itself as upon the firmest data of experience.

10. *The Moral Principle: Be Ready for Happiness*

Let us pause and reflect for a moment.

Thus far in answer to the question: what paths lead to the highest values? we have discovered at least that the guide to them is found in the social impulses. This does not answer the question completely, for further sign-posts and indications will be required; but we put aside this point for a moment. Now, since those altruistic inclinations are, we said, identical with those from which "moral" behavior for the most part proceeds, the way sought is also that which leads to morality. But to the concept of morality, which we investigated in Chapter IV, there is joined an indefiniteness of no small degree. We found that those dispositions are called moral which human society *believes* are most advantageous to its general welfare. Hence the content of the concept depends not only upon the actual living conditions of society, but also upon the intelligence of the class which determines public opinion, and upon the richness of its experience. This confusion and relativity is unavoidable; it is one of those facts which confront the philosopher and make the concept of a good disposition as unclear as that of "good weather." There remain, of course, enough universal moral precepts concerning which there is no difference of opinion; and many of these are common to the most dissimilar of nations and eras (if the concept of an altruistic disposition did not possess such a universal significance, independently of the nature of the culture involved, we should not have been able to arrive at our present results). But it remains unsatisfying that the definition of morality by the *opinion* of society makes meaningless a question which the philosopher (here becoming a moralist) would very much like to ask: namely, whether what society holds to be moral really *is* so. The attempt of utilitarianism to make the question sensible and subject to a decision miscarried, because the *real* "greatest happiness of the greatest number" is not a tangible concept (Chapter IV).

We now see the great advantage of our formulation of the question. We did not begin by seeking the causes of "moral" dispositions, but sought the disposition which is most valuable for the agent himself, which, that is, leads with the greatest probability to his happiness; and thus we eliminated any reference to the opinions of society. And we excluded the intangible concept of happiness, replacing it by the concept of the *capacity* for happiness, with the clear realization that the matter concerns this alone. And thus, it seems to me, the otherwise disturbing relativity and confusion of the problem is removed in so far as this is at all possible. Now, perhaps, a little light can be thrown back upon such dubious concepts as the utilitarian concept of "general welfare." Here too, we should prefer to speak of the maximum *capacity* for happiness of a society, and consider it to exist when each individual has attained his greatest capacity for happiness. We must always refer to the individuals, because, strictly speaking, pleasure and pain, happiness and sorrow, exist only for them. With the most sharply defined question there would, perhaps, be given the possibility subsequently of speaking of a standard of morality, and of judging whether different moral views correspond to it or not. The philosopher could, for his purposes, *define* as moral that behavior by means of which an individual furthered his capacity for happiness, and could designate the precepts of society as "truly" moral if this criterion fitted them. We must not forget, however, that he would in this fashion establish nothing but a definition, at bottom arbitrary, as is every other. He cannot force one to accept it, and cannot elevate it into a "postulate." I would hold it practical to accept this definition, because the end it establishes is that which *de facto* is most highly valued by mankind.

The formulation of a "moral principle," too, would be possible on this basis; and it would run, "At all times be fit for happiness," or "Be ready for happiness."

Everyone knows, or experience teaches him as he grows older, that happiness seems to vanish in direct ratio to the eagerness with which it is pursued. One cannot pursue it, one cannot seek it; for it cannot be recognized from afar, and only unveils itself suddenly, when present. Happiness, those rare moments of life in which the world by a coincidence of apparently insignificant circumstances suddenly grows perfect, the contact of a warm hand, the look of crystal clear water, the song of a bird, how could one "strive" for such things? Nor does it depend upon these things, but only upon the soul's receptivity which they find awaiting them. It depends upon the capacity of the soul to respond to the proper vibration, upon its strings not having lost their tension by reason of the tones hitherto drawn from them, upon the approaches to the highest joys not being choked with filth. But for all of these, for the receptivity and *purity* of the soul, one can provide. He cannot attract happiness to himself, but he can so arrange his whole life that he is always ready to receive it, *if* it comes.

Therefore it seems to me that the idea of the capacity for happiness must everywhere be made central in ethics. And if a moral principle is needed it can only be one which rests upon this concept, as does the formula just proposed. Therefore it is truly amazing that readiness for happiness nowhere plays an important role in ethical systems; I cannot remember ever having come upon the concept in an important place, except in a pompous disguise which ill becomes it, and renders it unrecognizable. In Kant and others one finds it said that one should not strive for happiness, but should seek to be *worthy* of happiness. Very true! But what does it mean to be worthy of happiness? Does this word express some mysterious property of a man or of his conduct, a mysterious relation to a possible reward? Or is there here an all-too-human transference of meaning from daily life, where we call a man worthy of a thing if he does not abuse it? Very likely the latter. But then it is at once clear that the word means nothing but *capacity* for happiness. The man who is able to appropriate the value of valuable things in the form of intense feelings of joy makes just the right use of them. Nature is not miserly nor thrifty, and makes no condition to the loan of its favors except that one be *capable* of receiving them. To be capable of happiness *is* to be worthy of happiness. Whoever is able and ready to share in the joys of the world is invited to them.

11. *Morality without Renunciation*

A necessary condition of the capacity for happiness is the existence of inclinations in which the motive pleasure and pleasure of realization do not clash; and all conduct and motives which strengthen such inclinations are to be accepted as leading to the most valuable life. Experience teaches that these conditions are fulfilled by the social impulses, hence by those inclinations which have as their goal the joyful states of other creatures; with them there is the least probability that the joys of realization do not correspond to the motive pleasure. They are, if we use the philosophical definition of morality recommended upon p. 197, the moral impulses *par excellence*.

I am, in fact, of the opinion that those philosophers are quite right (they constitute the majority, I believe) who find the essence of moral dispositions in *altruism*. We recognized that its essence lies in *considerateness* for one's fellow men; in accommodation to and friendly understanding of their needs lies the very essence of the moral character, or at least that aspect which signifies the "performance of duties toward others." Considerateness consists in the constant restraint and restriction of the non-altruistic impulses; and one can perhaps conceive all civilization as the colossal process of this subjugation of egoism, as the powerful means which ultimately serves to bring about a harmony among the inclinations of all persons. Now, it would seem as if this must be a very painful process for the individual, because apparently it demands the partial suppression of impulses, calls for renunciation and resignation. But this is illusory, for such restriction is, quite apart from this, necessary and salutary for the individual, since the unrestricted development of these impulses (as we saw on p. 184) has very painful consequences, and does not therefore lead to the most valuable life in any case. This holds to such a degree that often the altruistic inclinations are far from sufficient, and other impulses must be added to hold the primitive forces in check. These impulses correspond to the "duties with respect to oneself," including chiefly the so-called "higher" enjoyments: pleasure in knowledge and in beauty, or the joy in exceptional performances of all sorts (that is, in manual skill, in sport, and competition).

As soon as the altruistic and the last-mentioned

"higher" impulses are developed to a sufficient degree the process of subjugation is completed, and there is no longer any talk of "renunciation"; for proper conduct (that is, conduct which makes one ready for happiness) now flows quite of itself from the harmonious nature of the man. He no longer falls into "temptation"; "moral struggles" no longer occur in him; that is, the dangerous ends-in-view, which could seduce him from his path, no longer have as powerful a pleasure tone as do the opposing inclinations, and are suppressed by the latter. There is no longer required a strong excitation of pain to deter him from these ends—pain heretofore in part threatened from without by natural or artificial sanctions, and in part from within by "conscience," whose innermost component is doubtless nothing but the fear of injuring one's capacity for happiness, one's purity. To be sure, before this stage is reached in which the good is done "willingly," long periods of the development of civilization must pass, during which strong feelings of pain are necessary for the motivation of good behavior, so that it results only from the "compulsion" of duty and conscience (Kant, too, described the obedience to duty as unpleasant); but it would be a perversion to see the essence of morality in this, and to wish to find morality only where compulsion and conflicts trouble the soul. This is characteristic rather of the lower levels; the highest level of morality is the peace of "innocence."

This is, of course, wholly attained by no one. And

thus civilization works ceaselessly with all its means
to establish motives for altruistic conduct; and, rightly,
also lays much stress upon the *outer* form of considerateness, politeness and good manners, which, established by suggestion and custom, are able, by penetrating from the surface inwards, to influence important inclinations in no small degree.

The social impulses stand so much in the foreground
for moral behavior that in comparison the encourage-
ment given by the other impulses which increase the
capacity for happiness (scientific, aesthetic, and so
forth) plays a minor role. The little said regarding
them may suffice.

In them and in the altruistic inclinations lie the
roots of the most valuable conduct. That, in rough
outline, is the answer to the fundamental question of
ethics.

12. *Personality and Kindness*

But, with respect to the altruistic inclinations, we
must consider briefly an objection which the reader
must have long since had at the tip of his tongue.
The unrestricted development of such inclinations, he
will say, can certainly not lead to the valuable, and will
not, in fact, be considered moral. To respect every
desire of one's neighbor, to give in to every sympathetic
impulse results, finally, neither in the highest measure
of joy for the individual himself, nor indeed for the

others; in such a case one no longer speaks of kindness, but of *weakness*.

This is correct; and we must add a supplement in order to distinguish genuine kindness from the superficial variety which is nothing but lack of strength, and which is injurious to the capacity for happiness. What we have here is a special case of a general kind of disposition which exists whenever a man easily gives in to impulses of the moment, without, so to speak, first consulting the other impulses. In such a case the single dispositions are but loosely joined together, as it were; they can be excited separately, without the others thereby coming into play. The unity which constitutes a strong character is lacking. In a strong character it is as if the inclinations were all directed from one fixed center; every act has *consequences*. These are actually generated in the following manner: the separate dispositions hinder or favor one another, so that a definite orientation of the will seems to arise; they constitute a firmly knit system, a hierarchy, whose parts cannot be disturbed without the others responding. The *whole* man, as it were, enters into each act; and this constitutes the firmness and consequential nature of his character. To this is opposed instability and fickleness, which evidently have their causes in the fact that the separate inclinations are relatively more independent of one another; so that, as we say, the right hand knows not what the left hand does. The necessary mutual influence and correction is lacking. However, the intellect can be of some assistance here, for by means of a fitting association of ideas it sometimes sees to the excitation of the proper corrective impulse.

Thus, for instance, a man can be cruel and ambitious without his altruistic inclinations interfering. And the latter can occasionally come into play, and then we tend to say: at bottom he is not a bad man, but a weak man. If another lacks the evil inclinations and is driven by altruistic impulses which do not work in harmony, we say: he is good-natured, but weak. Weakness, therefore, is nothing but disorder, the lack of a hierarchical system among the impulses.

But if a firm order does exist, then out of good nature comes true kindness, which does not give ear to every request, does not raise every weakling to his feet, but first encourages him to rise of his own strength. Farther-seeing social inclinations stand over the shortsighted, helping and hindering; together they constitute a harmonious system, which gives to all conduct that peculiar aspect of being under control which distinguishes the strong character. Hence, when the social inclinations of a person are detrimental to his capacity for happiness, what is required is not their weakening, but, much rather, to order and bring them together into a system. Ethics is but little concerned with isolated inclinations apart from the others; what is important is their coöperation. And thus we see substantiated Shaftesbury's old truth, that in the moral character there exists a *harmony* of different inclinations. Together they form a balanced system. A man must react as a whole to every influence, never with only a small part of himself. In this way is developed that directness and consistency of life without which the capacity for the highest happiness is unthinkable.

If we group the totality of the altruistic impulses under the name of *kindness,* and designate the firm interconnection of all impulses as *personality,* then we may say that personality and kindness are the basic conditions of a valuable existence.

13. *Ethics of Duty and Ethics of Kindness*

Two views stand sharply opposed in recent ethics. According to the first, moral values have nothing to do with pleasure and pain; all natural inclinations belong to man's animal nature, and he rises above this only if his acts are not determined by the natural feelings of pleasure and pain, but by those higher values. According to the second view, moral behavior, also, has its origin in pleasure and pain; man is noble because he *enjoys* such behavior; the moral values rank so high because they signify the highest joys; the values do not stand above him but reside within him; it is *natural* for him to be good.

In the preceding observations I have quite unambiguously and, as I think, with perfect consistency sided with the second view, and have defended its standpoint in the analysis of the first. I have attempted to answer the ethical questions with constant reference to the answers given by the advocates of that view; indeed it often appeared to me that by far the greater part of our discussion was made necessary only by the existence of this first view, and that everything that was otherwise to be said in favor of the other standpoint must appear really trivial and self-evident to the reader.

We can set the two standpoints in opposition as the ethics of duty and the ethics of kindness, and in conclusion once more compare their essential characteristics.

The ethics of duty arises from the desire to place the foundation of morals upon absolutely firm ground, or perhaps even to make a foundation superfluous by positing morality itself as absolutely certain.

We have had to renounce any *absolutely* certain ground, for we were able to show only that a good person would in all *probability* live a most valuable life. But this is a sacrifice that every empirical ethics must make to *truth;* and it is at least a foundation, while the ethics of duty ultimately contents itself with mere asseverations. In addition, the sacrifice has no practical significance, for in life, indeed ultimately in science as well, we deal always with probabilities only. Moral rules, too, must refer to the average. We must equip a locomotive with great power even though it can become extremely dangerous if the switch is set improperly; we must tell the child to keep to the walk and out of the street, even though this advice may prove fatal if by chance a tile should fall from the roof. Theoretically we must, of course, grant (and we can reproach the empiristic ethical theories with lacking the spirit to make this admission) that cases occur (but very rarely) in which obedience to moral commandments clearly would *not* lead to the highest possible joy (for example, in the case of a person mortally ill, for whom it would no longer make sense to preserve his capacity for happiness); but it is one of the imperfections of the world, to be accepted with the others, that in such extreme cases morality becomes valueless.

Thus the renunciation of an absolute foundation becomes easy for us; it is indeed no sacrifice to give up the unattainable.

According to our view one who does the good because of duty stands on a lower level than one who does it because of an inclination, to whom it has become quite natural; and if we must speak of morality only in the first case, then all of our endeavors should be bent upon making morality superfluous. Instead of holding with Kant we agree with Marcus Aurelius, who said: in the stage of perfection "thou wilt do what is right, not because it is proper, but because thereby thou givest thyself pleasure."

The ethics of duty has known well how to make use of the intensity of the moral feelings, of the exalted nature of morality. It arouses these feelings in the reader so that he is ashamed of questioning too penetratingly into the foundations of morality (yet this is his sole task, as a philosophical investigator). The most frequently cited passage in the Kantian ethics is an example of the appeal to the reader's feelings. The passage, which, to be sure, has a kind of beauty, runs: "Duty, thou exalted great name, that containest nothing in thee amiable or ingratiating, but demandest submission; yet to bend the will dost menace naught, which were but to arouse natural aversion and fear; only a law dost thou establish, that of itself finds entrance into feeling, and yet acquires a reluctant reverence (if not always obedience) before which all inclinations are silent, though in secret they are opposed; what thy worthy origin, and where find the root of thy noble descent, which proudly resists all kinship with the inclinations, from which root derives the inflexible condition of that value men alone can give themselves?"

It is obvious that the ethics of kindness, if it wished, could make exactly the same use of the exalted nature of moral feelings; for it emphasizes the emotional character of morality much more. It can only be to its credit that morality is thus, in general, drawn closer to humanity. Hence the philosopher of kindness could direct an apostrophe to kindness, which could be patterned after the Kantian hymn to duty, word for word, and would run as follows:

Kindness, thou dear great name, that containest nothing in thee demanding loveless esteem, but prayest to be followed; thou dost not menace and needst not establish any law, but of thyself findest entrance into feeling, and willingly art revered; whose smile disarms all sister inclinations; thou art so glorious that we need not ask after thy descent, for whatever be thy origin it is ennobled through thee!

Index

Catalog
of
DOVER BOOKS

BOOKS EXPLAINING SCIENCE

(Note: The books listed under this category are general introductions, surveys, reviews, and non-technical expositions of science for the interested layman or scientist who wishes to brush up. Dover also publishes the largest list of inexpensive reprints of books on intermediate and higher mathematics, mathematical physics, engineering, chemistry, astronomy, etc., for the professional mathematician or scientist. For our complete Science Catalog, write Dept. catrr., Dover Publications, Inc., 180 Varick Street, New York 14, N. Y.)

CONCERNING THE NATURE OF THINGS, Sir William- Bragg. Royal Institute Christmas Lectures by Nobel Laureate. Excellent plain-language introduction to gases, molecules, crystal structure, etc. explains "building blocks" of universe, basic properties of matter, with simplest, clearest examples, demonstrations. 32pp. of photos; 57ˑfigures. 244pp. 5⅜ x 8.
T31 Paperbound $1.35

MATTER AND LIGHT, THE NEW PHYSICS, Louis de Broglie. Non-technical explanations by a Nobel Laureate of electro-magnetic theory, relativity, wave mechanics, quantum physics, philosophies of science, etc. Simple, yet accurate introduction to work of Planck, Bohr, Einstein, other modern physicists. Only 2 of 12 chapters require mathematics. 300pp. 5⅜ x 8.
T35 Paperbound $1.60

THE COMMON SENSE OF THE EXACT SCIENCES, W. K. Clifford. For 70 years, Clifford's work has been acclaimed as one of the clearest, yet most precise introductions to mathematical symbolism, measurement, surface boundaries, position, space, motion, mass and force, etc. Prefaces by Bertrand Russell and Karl Pearson. Introduction by James Newman. 130 figures. 249pp. 5⅜ x 8.
T61 Paperbound $1.60

THE NATURE OF LIGHT AND COLOUR IN THE OPEN AIR, M. Minnaert. What causes mirages? haloes? "multiple" suns and moons? Professor Minnaert explains these and hundreds of other fascinating natural optical phenomena in simple terms, tells how to observe them, suggests hundreds of experiments. 200 illus; 42 photos. xvi + 362pp.
T196 Paperbound $1ˑ95

SPINNING TOPS AND GYROSCOPIC MOTION, John Perry. Classic elementary text on dynamics of rotation treats gyroscopes, tops, how quasi-rigidity is induced in paper disks, smoke rings, chains, etc, by rapid motion, precession, earth's motion, etc. Contains many easy-to-perform experiments. Appendix on practical uses of gyroscopes. 62 figures. 128pp.
T416 Paperbound $1.00

A CONCISE HISTORY OF MATHEMATICS, D. Struik. This lucid, easily followed history of mathematics from the Ancient Near East to modern times requires no mathematical background itself, yet introduces both mathematicians and laymen to basic concepts and discoveries and the men who made them. Contains a collection of 31 portraits of eminent mathematicians. Bibliography. xix + 299pp. 5⅜ x 8.
T255 Paperbound $1.75

THE RESTLESS UNIVERSE, Max Born. A remarkably clear, thorough exposition of gases, electrons, ions, waves and particles, electronic structure of the atom, nuclear physics, written for the layman by a Nobel Laureate. "Much ·more thorough and deep than most attempts . . . easy and delightful," CHEMICAL AND ENGINEERING NEWS. Includes 7 animated sequences showing motion of molecules, alpha particles, etc. 11 full-page plates of photographs. Total of nearly 600 illus. 315pp. 6⅛ x 9¼.
T412 Paperbound $2.00

WHAT IS SCIENCE?, N. Campbell. The role of experiment, the function of mathematics, the nature of scientific laws, the limitations of science, and many other provocative topics are explored without technicalities by an eminent scientist. "Still an excellent introduction to scientific philosophy," H. Margenau in PHYSICS TODAY. 192pp. 5⅜ x 8.
S43 Paperbound $1.25

FADS AND FALLACIES IN THE NAME OF SCIENCE, Martin Gardner. The standard account of the various cults, quack systems and delusions which have recently masqueraded as science: hollow earth theory, Atlantis, dianetics, Reich's orgone theory, flying saucers, Bridey Murphy, psionics, irridiagnosis, many other fascinating fallacies that deluded tens of thousands. "Should be read by everyone, scientist and non-scientist alike," R. T. Birge, Prof. Emeritus, Univ. of California; Former President, American Physical Society. Formerly titled, "In the Name of Science." Revised and enlarged edition. x + 365pp. 5⅜ x 8.
T394 Paperbound **$1.50**

THE STUDY OF THE HISTORY OF MATHEMATICS, THE STUDY OF THE HISTORY OF SCIENCE, G. Sarton. Two books bound as one. Both volumes are standard introductions to their fields by an eminent science historian. They discuss problems of historical research, teaching, pitfalls, other matters of interest to the historically oriented writer, teacher, or student. Both have extensive bibliographies. 10 illustrations. 188pp. 5⅜ x 8.   T240 Paperbound **$1.25**

THE PRINCIPLES OF SCIENCE, W. S. Jevons. Unabridged reprinting of a milestone in the development of symbolic logic and other subjects concerning scientific methodology, probability, inferential validity, etc. Also describes Jevons' "logic machine," an early precursor of modern electronic calculators. Preface by E. Nagel. 839pp. 5⅜ x 8.   S446 Paperbound **$2.98**

SCIENCE THEORY AND MAN, Erwin Schroedinger. Complete, unabridged reprinting of "Science and the Human Temperament" plus an additional essay "What is an Elementary Particle?" Nobel Laureate Schroedinger discusses many aspects of modern physics from novel points of view which provide unusual insights for both laymen and physicists. 192 pp. 5⅜ x 8.
T428 Paperbound **$1.35**

BRIDGES AND THEIR BUILDERS, D. B. Steinman & S. R. Watson. Information about ancient, medieval, modern bridges; how they were built; who built them; the structural principles employed; the materials they are built of; etc. Written by one of the world's leading authorities on bridge design and construction. New, revised, expanded edition. 23 photos; 26 line drawings, xvii + 401pp. 5⅜ x 8.   T431 Paperbound **$1.95**

HISTORY OF MATHEMATICS, D. E. Smith. Most comprehensive non-technical history of math in English. In two volumes. Vol. I: A chronological examination of the growth of mathematics from primitive concepts up to 1900. Vol. II: The development of ideas in specific fields and areas, up through elementary calculus. The lives and works of over a thousand mathematicians are covered; thousands of specific historical problems and their solutions are clearly explained. Total of 510 illustrations, 1355pp. 5⅜ x 8. Set boxed in attractive container.   T429, T430 Paperbound, the set **$5.00**

PHILOSOPHY AND THE PHYSICISTS, L. S. Stebbing. A philosopher examines the philosophical implications of modern science by posing a lively critical attack on the popular science expositions of Sir James Jeans and Arthur Eddington. xvi + 295pp. 5⅜ x 8.
T480 Paperbound **$1.65**

ON MATHEMATICS AND MATHEMATICIANS, R. E. Moritz. The first collection of quotations by and about mathematicians in English. 1140 anecdotes, aphorisms, definitions, speculations, etc. give both mathematicians and layman stimulating new insights into what mathematics is, and into the personalities of the great mathematicians from Archimedes to Euler, Gauss, Klein, Weierstrass. Invaluable to teachers, writers. Extensive cross index. 410pp. 5⅜ x 8.
T489 Paperbound **$1.95**

NATURAL SCIENCE, BIOLOGY, GEOLOGY, TRAVEL

A SHORT HISTORY OF ANATOMY AND PHYSIOLOGY FROM THE GREEKS TO HARVEY, C. Singer. A great medical historian's fascinating intermediate account of the slow advance of anatomical and physiological knowledge from pre-scientific times to Vesalius, Harvey. 139 unusually interesting illustrations. 221pp. 5⅜ x 8.   T389 Paperbound **$1.75**

THE BEHAVIOUR AND SOCIAL LIFE OF HONEYBEES, Ronald Ribbands. The most comprehensive, lucid and authoritative book on bee habits, communication, duties, cell life, motivations, etc. "A MUST for every scientist, experimenter, and educator, and a happy and valuable selection for all interested in the honeybee," AMERICAN BEE JOURNAL. 690-item bibliography. 127 illus.; 11 photographic plates. 352pp. 5⅜ x 8⅜.   S410 Clothbound **$4.50**

TRAVELS OF WILLIAM BARTRAM, edited by Mark Van Doren. One of the 18th century's most delightful books, and one of the few first-hand sources of information about American geography, natural history, and anthropology of American Indian tribes of the time. "The mind of a scientist with the soul of a poet," John Livingston Lowes. 13 original illustrations, maps. Introduction by Mark Van Doren. 448pp. 5⅜ x 8.   T326 Paperbound **$2.00**

STUDIES ON THE STRUCTURE AND DEVELOPMENT OF VERTEBRATES, Edwin Goodrich. The definitive study of the skeleton, fins and limbs, head region, divisions of the body cavity, vascular, respiratory, excretory systems, etc., of vertebrates from fish to higher mammals, by the greatest comparative anatomist of recent times. "The standard textbook," JOURNAL OF ANATOMY. 754 illus. 69-page biographical study. 1186-item bibliography. 2 vols. Total of 906pp. 5⅜ x 8.   Vol. I: S449 Paperbound **$2.50**
Vol. II: S450 Paperbound **$2.50**

DOVER BOOKS

THE BIRTH AND DEVELOPMENT OF THE GEOLOGICAL SCIENCES, F. D. Adams. The most complete and thorough history of the earth sciences in print. Covers over 300 geological thinkers and systems; treats fossils, theories of stone growth, paleontology, earthquakes, vulcanists vs. neptunists, odd theories, etc. 91 illustrations, including medieval, Renaissance wood cuts, etc. 632 footnotes and bibliographic notes. 511pp. 308pp. 5⅜ x 8. **T5 Paperbound $2.00**

FROM MAGIC TO SCIENCE, Charles Singer. A close study of aspects of medical science from the Roman Empire through the Renaissance. The sections on early herbals, and "The Visions of Hildegarde of Bingen," are probably the best studies of these subjects available. 158 unusual classic and medieval illustrations. xxvii + 365pp. 5⅜ x 8. **T390 Paperbound $2.00**

SAILING ALONE AROUND THE WORLD, Captain Joshua Slocum. Captain Slocum's personal account of his single-handed voyage around the world in a 34-foot boat he rebuilt himself. A classic of both seamanship and descriptive writing. "A nautical equivalent of Thoreau's account," Van Wyck Brooks. 67 illus. 308pp. 5⅜ x 8. **T326 Paperbound $1.00**

TREES OF THE EASTERN AND CENTRAL UNITED STATES AND CANADA, W. M. Harlow. Standard middle-level guide designed to help you know the characteristics of Eastern trees and identify them at sight by means of an 8-page synoptic key. More than 600 drawings and photographs of twigs, leaves, fruit, other features. xiii + 288pp. 4⅝ x 6½.
T395 Paperbound $1.35

FRUIT KEY AND TWIG KEY ("Fruit Key to Northeastern Trees," "Twig Key to Deciduous Woody Plants of Eastern North America"), **W. M. Harlow.** Identify trees in fall, winter, spring. Easy-to-use, synoptic keys, with photographs of every twig and fruit identified. Covers 120 different fruits, 160 different twigs. Over 350 photos. Bibliographies. Glossaries. Total of 143pp. 5⅝ x 8⅜. **T511 Paperbound $1.25**

INTRODUCTION TO THE STUDY OF EXPERIMENTAL MEDICINE, Claude Bernard. This classic records Bernard's far-reaching efforts to transform physiology into an exact science. It covers problems of vivisection, the limits of physiological experiment, hypotheses in medical experimentation, hundreds of others. Many of his own famous experiments on the liver, the pancreas, etc., are used as examples. Foreword by I. B. Cohen. xxv + 266pp. 5⅜ x 8.
T400 Paperbound $1.50

THE ORIGIN OF LIFE, A. I. Oparin. The first modern statement that life evolved from complex nitro-carbon compounds, carefully presented according to modern biochemical knowledge of primary colloids, organic molecules, etc. Begins with historical introduction to the problem of the origin of life. Bibliography. xxv + 270pp. 5⅜ x 8. **S213 Paperbound $1.75**

A HISTORY OF ASTRONOMY FROM THALES TO KEPLER, J. L. E. Dreyer. The only work in English which provides a detailed picture of man's cosmological views from Egypt, Babylonia, Greece, and Alexandria to Copernicus, Tycho Brahe and Kepler. "Standard reference on Greek astronomy and the Copernican revolution," SKY AND TELESCOPE. Formerly called "A History of Planetary Systems From Thales to Kepler." Bibliography. 21 diagrams. xvii + 430pp. 5⅜ x 8.
S79 Paperbound $1.98

URANIUM PROSPECTING, H. L. Barnes. A professional geologist tells you what you need to know. Hundreds of facts about minerals, tests, detectors, sampling, assays, claiming, developing, government regulations, etc. Glossary of technical terms. Annotated bibliography. x + 117pp. 5⅜ x 8. **T309 Paperbound $1.00**

DE RE METALLICA, Georgius Agricola. All 12 books of this 400 year old classic on metals and metal production, fully annotated, and containing all 289 of the 16th century woodcuts which made the original an artistic masterpiece. A superb gift for geologists, engineers, libraries, artists, historians. Translated by Herbert Hoover & L. H. Hoover. Bibliography, survey of ancient authors. 289 illustrations of the excavating, assaying, smelting, refining, and countless other metal production operations described in the text. 672pp. 6¾ x 10¾. Deluxe library edition. **S6 Clothbound $10.00**

DE MAGNETE, William Gilbert. A landmark of science by the man who first used the word "electricity," distinguished between static electricity and magnetism, and founded a new science. P. F. Mottelay translation. 90 figures. lix + 368pp. 5⅜ x 8. **S470 Paperbound $2.00**

THE AUTOBIOGRAPHY OF CHARLES DARWIN AND SELECTED LETTERS, Francis Darwin, ed. Fascinating documents on Darwin's early life, the voyage of the "Beagle," the discovery of evolution, Darwin's thought on mimicry, plant development, vivisection, evolution, many other subjects. Letters to Henslow, Lyell, Hooker, Wallace, Kingsley, etc. Appendix. 365pp. 5⅜ x 8. **T479 Paperbound $1.65**

A WAY OF LIFE AND OTHER SELECTED WRITINGS OF SIR WILLIAM OSLER. 16 of the great physician, teacher and humanist's most inspiring writings on a practical philosophy of life, science and the humanities, and the history of medicine. 5 photographs. Introduction by G. L. Keynes, M.D., F.R.C.S. xx + 278pp. 5⅜ x 8. **T488 Paperbound $1.50**

WORLD DRAMA, B. H. Clark. 46 plays from Ancient Greece, Rome, to India, China, Japan. Plays by Aeschylus, Sophocles, Euripides, Aristophanes, Plautus, Marlowe, Jonson, Farquhar, Goldsmith, Cervantes, Molière, Dumas, Goethe, Schiller, Ibsen, many others. One of the most comprehensive collections of important plays from all literature available in English. Over ⅓ of this material is unavailable in any other current edition. Reading lists. 2 volumes. Total of 1364pp. 5⅜ x 8.   Vol. I, T57 Paperbound **$2.00**
                                                                    Vol. II, T59 Paperbound **$2.00**

MASTERS OF THE DRAMA, John Gassner. The most comprehensive history of the drama in print. Covers more than 800 dramatists and over 2000 plays from the Greeks to modern Western, Near Eastern, Oriental drama. Plot summaries, theatre history, etc. "Best of its kind in English," NEW REPUBLIC. 35 pages of bibliography. 77 photos and drawings. Deluxe edition. xxii + 890pp. 5⅜ x 8.   T100 Clothbound **$5.95**

THE DRAMA OF LUIGI PIRANDELLO, D. Vittorini. All 38 of Pirandello's plays (to 1935) summarized and analyzed in terms of symbolic techniques, plot structure, etc. The only authorized work. Foreword by Pirandello. Biography. Bibliography. xiii + 350pp. 5⅜ x 8.
                                                                    T435 Paperbound **$1.98**

ARISTOTLE'S THEORY OF POETRY AND THE FINE ARTS, S. H. Butcher, ed. The celebrated "Butcher translation" faced page by page with the Greek text; Butcher's 300-page introduction to Greek poetic, dramatic thought. Modern Aristotelian criticism discussed by John Gassner. lxxvi + 421pp. 5⅜ x 8.
                                                                    T42 Paperbound **$2.00**

EUGENE O'NEILL: THE MAN AND HIS PLAYS, B. H. Clark. The first published source-book on O'Neill's life and work. Analyzes each play from the early THE WEB to THE ICEMAN COMETH. Supplies much information about environmental and dramatic influences. ix + 182pp. 5⅜ x 8.   T379 Paperbound **$1.25**

INTRODUCTION TO ENGLISH LITERATURE, B. Dobrée, ed. Most compendious literary aid in its price range. Extensive, categorized bibliography (with entries up to 1949) of more than 5,000 poets, dramatists, novelists, as well as historians, philosophers, economists, religious writers, travellers, and scientists of literary stature. Information about manuscripts, important biographical data. Critical, historical, background works not simply listed, but evaluated. Each volume also contains a long introduction to the period it covers.

Vol. I: **THE BEGINNINGS OF ENGLISH LITERATURE TO SKELTON, 1509, W. L. Renwick. H. Orton.** 450pp. 5⅛ x 7⅛.   T75 Clothbound **$3.50**
                                                                    T76 Clothbound **$3.50**
Vol. II: **THE ENGLISH RENAISSANCE, 1510-1688, V. de Sola Pinto.** 381pp. 5⅛ x 7⅛.
                                                                    T76 Clothbound **$3.50**
Vol. III: **THE AUGUSTANS AND ROMANTICS, 1689-1830, H. Dyson, J. Butt.** 320pp. 5⅛ x-7⅛.
                                                                    T77 Clothbound **$3.50**
Vol. IV: **THE VICTORIANS AND AFTER, 1830-1914, E. Batho, B. Dobrée.** 360pp. 5⅛ x 7⅛.
                                                                    T78 Clothbound **$3.50**

EPIC AND ROMANCE, W. P. Ker. The standard survey of Medieval epic and romance by a foremost authority on Medieval literature. Covers historical background, plot, literary analysis, significance of Teutonic epics, Icelandic sagas, Beowulf, French chansons de geste, the Niebelungenlied, Arthurian romances, much more. 422pp. 5⅜ x 8.   T355 Paperbound **$1.95**

THE HEART OF EMERSON'S JOURNALS, Bliss Perry, ed. Emerson's most intimate thoughts, impressions, records of conversations with Channing, Hawthorne, Thoreau, etc., carefully chosen from the 10 volumes of The Journals. "The essays do not reveal the power of Emerson's mind . . .as do these hasty and informal writings," N. Y. TIMES. Preface by B. Perry. 370pp. 5⅜ x 8.   T447 Paperbound **$1.85**

A SOURCE BOOK IN THEATRICAL HISTORY, A. M. Nagler. (Formerly, "Sources of Theatrical History.") Over 300 selected passages by contemporary observers tell about styles of acting, direction, make-up, scene designing, etc., in the theatre's great periods from ancient Greece to the Théâtre Libre. "Indispensable complement to the study of drama," EDUCATIONAL THEATRE JOURNAL. Prof. Nagler, Yale Univ. School of Drama, also supplies notes, references. 85 illustrations. 611pp. 5⅜ x 8.   T515 Paperbound **$2.75**

THE ART OF THE STORY-TELLER, M. L. Shedlock. Regarded as the finest, most helpful book on telling stories to children, by a great story-teller. How to catch, hold, recapture attention; how to choose material; many other aspects. Also includes: a 99-page selection of Miss Shedlock's most successful stories; extensive bibliography of other stories. xxi + 320pp. 5⅜ x 8.   T245 Clothbound **$3.50**

THE DEVIL'S DICTIONARY, Ambrose Bierce. Over 1000 short, ironic definitions in alphabetical order, by America's greatest satirist in the classical tradition. "Some of the most gorgeous witticisms in the English language," H. L. Mencken. 144pp. 5⅜ x 8. T487 Paperbound **$1.00**

DOVER BOOKS

MUSIC

A DICTIONARY OF HYMNOLOGY, John Julian. More than 30,000 entries on individual hymns, their authorship, textual variations, location of texts, dates and circumstances of composition, denominational and ritual usages, the biographies of more than 9,000 hymn writers, essays on important topics such as children's hymns and Christmas carols, and hundreds of thousands of other important facts about hymns which are virtually impossible to find anywhere else. Convenient alphabetical listing, and a 200-page double-columned index of first lines enable you to track down virtually any hymn ever written. Total of 1786pp. 6¼ x 9¼. 2 volumes.   T133. The Set, Clothbound **$15.00**

STRUCTURAL HEARING, TONAL COHERENCE IN MUSIC, Felix Salzer. Extends the well-known Schenker approach to include modern music, music of the middle ages, and Renaissance music. Explores the phenomenon of tonal organization by discussing more than 500 compositions, and offers unusual new insights into the theory of composition and musical relationships. "The foundation on which all teaching in music theory has been based at this college," Leopold Mannes, President, The Mannes College of Music. Total of 658pp. 6½ x 9¼. 2 volumes.   S418 The set, Clothbound **$8.00**

A GENERAL HISTORY OF MUSIC, Charles Burney. The complete history of music from the Greeks up to 1789 by the 18th century musical historian who personally knew the great Baroque composers. Covers sacred and secular, vocal and instrumental, operatic and symphonic music; treats theory, notation, forms, instruments; discusses composers, performers, important works. Invaluable as a source of information on the period for students, historians, musicians. "Surprisingly few of Burney's statements have been invalidated by modern research . . . still of great value," NEW YORK TIMES. Edited and corrected by Frank Mercer. 35 figures. 1915pp. 5½ x 8½. 2 volumes.   T36 The set, Clothbound **$12.50**

JOHANN SEBASTIAN BACH, Phillip Spitta. Recognized as one of the greatest accomplishments of musical scholarship and far and away the definitive coverage of Bach's works. Hundreds of individual pieces are analyzed. Major works, such as the B Minor Mass and the St. Matthew Passion are examined in minute detail. Spitta also deals with the works of Buxtehude, Pachelbel, and others of the period. Can be read with profit even by those without a knowledge of the technicalities of musical composition. "Unchallenged as the last word on one of the supreme geniuses of music," John Barkham, SATURDAY REVIEW SYNDICATE. Total of 1819pp. 5⅜ x 8. 2 volumes.   T252 The set, Clothbound **$10.00**

HISTORY

THE IDEA OF PROGRESS, J. B. Bury. Prof. Bury traces the evolution of a central concept of Western civilization in Greek, Roman, Medieval, and Renaissance thought to its flowering in the 17th and 18th centuries. Introduction by Charles Beard. xl + 357pp. 5⅜ x 8.
     T39 Clothbound **$3.95**
     T40 Paperbound **$1.95**

THE ANCIENT GREEK HISTORIANS, J. B. Bury. Greek historians such as Herodotus, Thucydides, Xenophon; Roman historians such as Tacitus, Caesar, Livy; scores of others fully analyzed in terms of sources, concepts, influences, etc., by a great scholar and historian. 291pp. 5⅜ x 8.   T397 Paperbound **$1.50**

HISTORY OF THE LATER ROMAN EMPIRE, J. B. Bury. The standard work on the Byzantine Empire from 395 A.D. to the death of Justinian in 565 A.D., by the leading Byzantine scholar of our time. Covers political, social, cultural, theological, military history. Quotes contemporary documents extensively. "Most unlikely that it will ever be superseded," Glanville Downey, Dumbarton Oaks Research Library. Genealogical tables. 5 maps. Bibliography. 2 vols. Total of 965pp. 5⅜ x 8.   T398, T399 Paperbound, the set **$4.00**

GARDNER'S PHOTOGRAPHIC SKETCH BOOK OF THE CIVIL WAR, Alexander Gardner. One of the rarest and most valuable Civil War photographic collections exactly reproduced for the first time since 1866. Scenes of Manassas, Bull Run, Harper's Ferry, Appomattox, Mechanicsville, Fredericksburg, Gettysburg, etc.; battle ruins, prisons, arsenals, a slave pen, fortifications; Lincoln on the field, officers, men, corpses. By one of the most famous pioneers in documentary photography. Original copies of the "Sketch Book" sold for $425 in 1952. Introduction by E. Bleiler. 100 full-page 7 x 10 photographs (original size). 244pp. 10¾ x 8½
     T476 Clothbound **$6.00**

THE WORLD'S GREAT SPEECHES, L. Copeland and L. Lamm, eds. 255 speeches from Pericles to Churchill, Dylan Thomas. Invaluable as a guide to speakers; fascinating as history past and present; a source of much difficult-to-find material. Includes an extensive section of informal and humorous speeches. 3 indices: Topic, Author, Nation. xx + 745pp. 5⅜ x 8.
     T468 Paperbound **$2.49**

FOUNDERS OF THE MIDDLE AGES, E. K. Rand. The best non-technical discussion of the transformation of Latin paganism into medieval civilization. Tertullian, Gregory, Jerome, Boethius, Augustine, the Neoplatonists, other crucial figures, philosophies examined. Excellent for the intelligent non-specialist. "Extraordinarily accurate," Richard McKeon, THE NATION. ix + 365pp. 5⅜ x 8.   T369 Paperbound **$1.85**

THE POLITICAL THOUGHT OF PLATO AND ARISTOTLE, Ernest Barker. The standard, comprehensive exposition of Greek political thought. Covers every aspect of the "Republic" and the "Politics" as well as minor writings, other philosophers, theorists of the period, and the later history of Greek political thought. Unabridged edition. 584pp. 5⅜ x 8.
T521 Paperbound **$1.85**

PHILOSOPHY

THE GIFT OF LANGUAGE, M. Schlauch. (Formerly, "The Gift of Tongues.") A sound, middle-level treatment of linguistic families, word histories, grammatical processes, semantics, language taboos, word-coining of Joyce, Cummings, Stein, etc. 232 bibliographical notes. 350pp. 5⅜ x 8.
T243 Paperbound **$1.85**

THE PHILOSOPHY OF HEGEL, W. T. Stace. The first work in English to give a complete and connected view of Hegel's entire system. Especially valuable to those who do not have time to study the highly complicated original texts, yet want an accurate presentation by a most reputable scholar of one of the most influential 19th century thinkers. Includes a 14 x 20 fold-out chart of Hegelian system. 536pp. 5⅜ x 8.
T254 Paperbound **$2.00**

ARISTOTLE, A. E. Taylor. A lucid, non-technical account of Aristotle written by a foremost Platonist. Covers life and works; thought on matter, form, causes, logic, God, physics, metaphysics, etc. Bibliography. New index compiled for this edition. 128pp. 5⅜ x 8.
T280 Paperbound **$1.00**

GUIDE TO PHILOSOPHY, C. E. M. Joad. This basic work describes the major philosophic problems and evaluates the answers propounded by great philosophers from the Greeks to Whitehead, Russell. "The finest introduction," BOSTON TRANSCRIPT. Bibliography, 592pp. 5⅜ x 8.
T297 Paperbound **$2.00**

LANGUAGE AND MYTH, E. Cassirer. Cassirer's brilliant demonstration that beneath both language and myth lies an unconscious "grammar" of experience whose categories and canons are not those of logical thought. Introduction and translation by Susanne Langer. Index. x + 103pp. 5⅜ x 8.
T51 Paperbound **$1.25**

SUBSTANCE AND FUNCTION, EINSTEIN'S THEORY OF RELATIVITY, E. Cassirer. This double volume contains the German philosopher's profound philosophical formulation of the differences between traditional logic and the new logic of science. Number, space, energy, relativity, many other topics are treated in detail. Authorized translation by W. C. and M. C. Swabey. xii + 465pp. 5⅜ x 8.
T50 Paperbound **$2.00**

THE PHILOSOPHICAL WORKS OF DESCARTES. The definitive English edition, in two volumes, of all major philosophical works and letters of René Descartes, father of modern philosophy of knowledge and science. Translated by E. S. Haldane and G. Ross. Introductory notes. Total of 842pp. 5⅜ x 8.
T71 Vol. 1, Paperbound **$2.00**
T72 Vol. 2, Paperbound **$2.00**

ESSAYS IN EXPERIMENTAL LOGIC, J. Dewey. Based upon Dewey's theory that knowledge implies a judgment which in turn implies an inquiry, these papers consider such topics as the thought of Bertrand Russell, pragmatism, the logic of values, antecedents of thought, data and meanings. 452pp. 5⅜ x 8.
T73 Paperbound **$1.95**

THE PHILOSOPHY OF HISTORY, G. W. F. Hegel. This classic of Western thought is Hegel's detailed formulation of the thesis that history is not chance but a rational process, the realization of the Spirit of Freedom. Translated and introduced by J. Sibree. Introduction by C. Hegel. Special introduction for this edition by Prof. Carl Friedrich, Harvard University. xxxix + 447pp. 5⅜ x 8.
T112 Paperbound **$1.85**

THE WILL TO BELIEVE and HUMAN IMMORTALITY, W. James. Two of James's most profound investigations of human belief in God and immortality, bound as one volume. Both are powerful expressions of James's views on chance vs. determinism, pluralism vs. monism, will and intellect, arguments for survival after death, etc. Two prefaces. 429pp. 5⅜ x 8.
T294 Clothbound **$3.75**
T291 Paperbound **$1.65**

INTRODUCTION TO SYMBOLIC LOGIC, S. Langer. A lucid, general introduction to modern logic, covering forms, classes, the use of symbols, the calculus of propositions, the Boole-Schroeder and the Russell-Whitehead systems, etc. "One of the clearest and simplest introductions," MATHEMATICS GAZETTE. Second, enlarged, revised edition. 368pp. 5⅜ x 8.
S164 Paperbound **$1.75**

MIND AND THE WORLD-ORDER, C. I. Lewis. Building upon the work of Peirce, James, and Dewey, Professor Lewis outlines a theory of knowledge in terms of "conceptual pragmatism," and demonstrates why the traditional understanding of the a priori must be abandoned. Appendices. xiv + 446pp. 5⅜ x 8.
T359 Paperbound **$1.95**

THE GUIDE FOR THE PERPLEXED, M. Maimonides One of the great philosophical works of all time, Maimonides' formulation of the meeting-ground between Old Testament and Aristotelian thought is essential to anyone interested in Jewish, Christian, and Moslem thought in the Middle Ages. 2nd revised edition of the Friedländer translation. Extensive introduction. lix + 414pp. 5⅜ x 8.
T351 Paperbound **$1.85**

DOVER BOOKS

THE PHILOSOPHICAL WRITINGS OF PEIRCE, J. Buchler, ed. (Formerly, "The Philosophy of Peirce.") This carefully integrated selection of Peirce's papers is considered the best coverage of the complete thought of one of the greatest philosophers of modern times. Covers Peirce's work on the theory of signs, pragmatism, epistemology, symbolic logic, the scientific method, chance, etc. xvi + 386pp. 5 ⅜ x 8. T216 Clothbound **$5.00**
T217 Paperbound **$1.95**

HISTORY OF ANCIENT PHILOSOPHY, W. Windelband. Considered the clearest survey of Greek and Roman philosophy. Examines Thales, Anaximander, Anaximenes, Heraclitus, the Eleatics, Empedocles, the Pythagoreans, the Sophists, Socrates, Democritus, Stoics, Epicureans, Sceptics, Neo-platonists, etc. 50 pages on Plato; 70 on Aristotle. 2nd German edition tr. by H. E. Cushman. xv + 393pp. 5⅜ x 8. T357 Paperbound **$1.75**

INTRODUCTION TO SYMBOLIC LOGIC AND ITS APPLICATIONS, R. Carnap. A comprehensive, rigorous introduction to modern logic by perhaps its greatest living master. Includes demonstrations of applications in mathematics, physics, biology. "Of the rank of a masterpiece," Z. für Mathematik und ihre Grenzgebiete. Over 300 exercises. xvi + 241pp. 5⅜ x 8. Clothbound **$4.00**
S453 Paperbound **$1.85**

SCEPTICISM AND ANIMAL FAITH, G. Santayana. Santayana's unusually lucid exposition of the difference between the independent existence of objects and the essence our mind attributes to them, and of the necessity of scepticism as a form of belief and animal faith as a necessary condition of knowledge. Discusses belief, memory, intuition, symbols, etc. xii + 314pp. 5⅜ x 8. T235 Clothbound **$3.50**
T236 Paperbound **$1.50**

THE ANALYSIS OF MATTER, B. Russell. With his usual brilliance, Russell analyzes physics, causality, scientific inference, Weyl's theory, tensors, invariants, periodicity, etc. in order to discover the basic concepts of scientific thought about matter. "Most thorough treatment of the subject," THE NATION. Introduction. 8 figures. viii + 408pp. 5⅜ x 8. T231 Paperbound **$1.95**

THE SENSE OF BEAUTY, G. Santayana. This important philosophical study of why, when, and how beauty appears, and what conditions must be fulfilled, is in itself a revelation of the beauty of language. "It is doubtful if a better treatment of the subject has since appeared," PEABODY JOURNAL. ix + 275pp. 5⅜ x 8. T238 Paperbound **$1.00**

THE CHIEF WORKS OF SPINOZA. In two volumes. Vol. I: The Theologico-Political Treatise and the Political Treatise. Vol. II: On the Improvement of Understanding, The Ethics, and Selected Letters. The permanent and enduring ideas in these works on God, the universe, religion, society, etc., have had tremendous impact on later philosophical works. Introduction. Total of 862pp. 5⅜ x 8. T249 Vol. I, Paperbound **$1.50**
T250 Vol. II, Paperbound **$1.50**

TRAGIC SENSE OF LIFE, M. de Unamuno. The acknowledged masterpiece of one of Spain's most influential thinkers. Between the despair at the inevitable death of man and all his works, and the desire for immortality, Unamuno finds a "saving incertitude." Called "a masterpiece," by the ENCYCLOPAEDIA BRITANNICA. xxx + 332pp. 5⅜ x 8. T257 Paperbound **$1.95**

EXPERIENCE AND NATURE, John Dewey. The enlarged, revised edition of the Paul Carus lectures (1925). One of Dewey's clearest presentations of the philosophy of empirical naturalism which reestablishes the continuity between "inner" experience and "outer" nature. These lectures are among the most significant ever delivered by an American philosopher. 457pp. 5⅜ x 8. T471 Paperbound **$1.85**

PHILOSOPHY AND CIVILIZATION IN THE MIDDLE AGES, M. de Wulf. A semi-popular survey of medieval intellectual life, religion, philosophy, science, the arts, etc. that covers feudalism vs. Catholicism, rise of the universities, mendicant orders, and similar topics. Bibliography. viii + 320pp. 5⅜ x 8. T284 Paperbound **$1.75**

AN INTRODUCTION TO SCHOLASTIC PHILOSOPHY, M. de Wulf. (Formerly, "Scholasticism Old and New.") Prof. de Wulf covers the central scholastic tradition from St. Anselm, Albertus Magnus, Thomas Aquinas, up to Suarez in the 17th century; and then treats the modern revival of scholasticism, the Louvain position, relations with Kantianism and positivism, etc. xvi + 271pp. 5⅜ x 8. T296 Clothbound **$3.50**
T283 Paperbound **$1.75**

A HISTORY OF MODERN PHILOSOPHY, H. Höffding. An exceptionally clear and detailed coverage of Western philosophy from the Renaissance to the end of the 19th century. Both major and minor figures are examined in terms of theory of knowledge, logic, cosmology, psychology. Covers Pomponazzi, Bodin, Boehme, Telesius, Bruno, Copernicus, Descartes, Spinoza, Hobbes, Locke, Hume, Kant, Fichte, Schopenhauer, Mill, Spencer, Langer, scores of others. A standard reference work. 2 volumes. Total of 1159pp. 5⅜ x 8. T117 Vol. 1, Paperbound **$2.00**
T118 Vol. 2, Paperbound **$2.00**

LANGUAGE, TRUTH AND LOGIC, A. J. Ayer. The first full-length development of Logical Posivitism in English. Building on the work of Schlick, Russell, Carnap, and the Vienna school, Ayer presents the tenets of one of the most important systems of modern philosophical thought. 160pp. 5⅜ x 8. T10 Paperbound **$1.25**

ORIENTALIA AND RELIGION

THE MYSTERIES OF MITHRA, F. Cumont. The great Belgian scholar's definitive study of the Persian mystery religion that almost vanquished Christianity in the ideological struggle for the Roman Empire. A masterpiece of scholarly detection that reconstructs secret doctrines, organization, rites. Mithraic art is discussed and analyzed. 70 illus. 239pp. 5⅜ x 8.
T323 Paperbound **$1.85**

CHRISTIAN AND ORIENTAL PHILOSOPHY OF ART. A. K. Coomaraswamy. The late art historian and orientalist discusses artistic symbolism, the role of traditional culture in enriching art, medieval art, folklore, philosophy of art, other similar topics. Bibliography. 148pp. 5⅜ x 8.
T378 Paperbound **$1.25**

TRANSFORMATION OF NATURE IN ART, A. K. Coomaraswamy. A basic work on Asiatic religious art. Includes discussions of religious art in Asia and Medieval Europe (exemplified by Meister Eckhart), the origin and use of images in Indian art, Indian Medieval aesthetic manuals, and other fascinating, little known topics. Glossaries of Sanskrit and Chinese terms. Bibliography. 41pp. of notes. 245pp. 5⅜ x 8.
T368 Paperbound **$1.75**

ORIENTAL RELIGIONS IN ROMAN PAGANISM, F. Cumont. This well-known study treats the ecstatic cults of Syria and Phrygia (Cybele, Attis, Adonis, their orgies and mutilatory rites); the mysteries of Egypt (Serapis, Isis, Osiris); Persian dualism; Mithraic cults; Hermes Trismegistus, Ishtar, Astarte, etc. and their influence on the religious thought of the Roman Empire. Introduction. 55pp. of notes; extensive bibliography. xxiv + 298pp. 5⅜ x 8.
T321 Paperbound **$1.75**

ANTHROPOLOGY, SOCIOLOGY, AND PSYCHOLOGY

PRIMITIVE MAN AS PHILOSOPHER, P. Radin. A standard anthropological work based on Radin's investigations of the Winnebago, Maori, Batak, Zuni, other primitive tribes. Describes primitive thought on the purpose of life, marital relations, death, personality, gods, etc. Extensive selections of õriginal primitive documents. Bibliography. xviii + 420pp. 5⅜ x 8.
T392 Paperbound **$2.00**

PRIMITIVE RELIGION, P. Radin. Radin's thoroughgoing treatment of supernatural beliefs, shamanism, initiations, religious expression, etc. in primitive societies. Arunta, Ashanti, Aztec, Bushman, Crow, Fijian, many other tribes examined. "Excellent," NATURE. New preface by the author. Bibliographic notes. x + 322pp. 5⅜ x 8.
T393 Paperbound **$1.85**

SEX IN PSYCHO-ANALYSIS, S. Ferenczi. (Formerly, "Contributions to Psycho-analysis.") 14 selected papers on impotence, transference, analysis and children, dreams, obscene words, homosexuality, paranoia, etc. by an associate of Freud. Also included: THE DEVELOPMENT OF PSYCHO-ANALYSIS, by Ferenczi and Otto Rank. Two books bound as one. Total of 406pp. 5⅜ x 8.
T324 Paperbound **$1.85**

THE PRINCIPLES OF PSYCHOLOGY, William James. The complete text of the famous "long course," one of the great books of Western thought. An almost incredible amount of information about psychological processes, the stream of consciousness, habit, time perception, memory, emotions, reason, consciousness of self, abnormal phenomena, and similar topics. Based on James's own discoveries integrated with the work of Descartes, Locke, Hume, Royce, Wundt, Berkeley, Lotse, Herbart, scores of others. "A classic of interpretation," PSYCHIATRIC QUARTERLY. 94 illus. 1408pp. 2 volumes. 5⅜ x 8.
T381 Vol. 1, Paperbound **$2.50**
T382 Vol. 2, Paperbound **$2.50**

THE POLISH PEASANT IN EUROPE AND AMERICA, W. I. Thomas, F. Znaniecki. Monumental sociological study of peasant primary groups (family and community) and the disruptions produced by·a new industrial system and emigration to America, by two of the foremost sociologists of recent times. One of the most important works in sociological thought. Includes hundreds of pages of primary documentation; point by point analysis of causes of social decay, breakdown of morality, crime, drunkenness, prostitution, etc. 2nd revised edition. 2 volumes. Total of 2250pp. 6 x 9.
T478 2 volume set, Clothbound **$12.50**

FOLKWAYS, W. G. Sumner. The great Yale sociologist's detailed exposition of thousands of social, sexual, and religious customs in hundreds of cultures from ancient Greece to Modern Western societies. Preface by A. G. Keller. Introduction by William Lyon Phelps. 705pp. 5⅜ x 8.
S508 Paperbound **$2.49**

BEYOND PSYCHOLOGY, Otto Rank. The author, an early associate of Freud, uses psychoanalytic techniques of myth-analysis to explore ultimates of human existence. Treats love, immortality, the soul, sexual identity, kingship, sources of state power, many other topics which illuminate the irrational basis of human existence. 291pp. 5⅜ x 8.
T485 Paperbound **$1.75**

ILLUSIONS AND DELUSIONS OF THE SUPERNATURAL AND THE OCCULT, D. H. Rawcliffe. A rational, scientific examination of crystal gazing, automatic writing, table turning, stigmata, the Indian rope trick, dowsing, telepathy, clairvoyance, ghosts, ESP, PK, thousands of other supposedly occult phenomena. Originally titled "The Psychology of the Occult." 14 illustrations. 551pp. 5⅜ x 8.
T503 Paperbound **$2.00**

DOVER BOOKS

YOGA: A SCIENTIFIC EVALUATION, Kovoor T. Behanan. A scientific study of the physiological and psychological effects of Yoga discipline, written under the auspices of the Yale University Institute of Human Relations. Foreword by W. A. Miles, Yale Univ. 17 photographs. 290pp. 5⅜ x 8. T505 Paperbound **$1.65**

HOAXES, C. D. MacDougall. Delightful, entertaining, yet scholarly exposition of how hoaxes start, why they succeed, documented with stories of hundreds of the most famous hoaxes. "A stupendous collection . . . and shrewd analysis, "NEW YORKER. New, revised edition. 54 photographs. 320pp. 5⅜ x 8. T465 Paperbound **$1.75**

CREATIVE POWER: THE EDUCATION OF YOUTH IN THE CREATIVE ARTS, Hughes Mearns. Named by the National Education Association as one of the 20 foremost books on education in recent times. Tells how to help children express themselves in drama, poetry, music, art, develop latent creative power. Should be read by every parent, teacher. New, enlarged, revised edition. Introduction. 272pp. 5⅜ x 8. T490 Paperbound **$1.50**

LANGUAGES

NEW RUSSIAN-ENGLISH, ENGLISH-RUSSIAN DICTIONARY, M. A. O'Brien. Over- 70,000 entries in new orthography! Idiomatic usages, colloquialisms. One of the few dictionaries that indicate accent changes in conjugation and declension. "One of the best," Prof. E. J. Simmons, Cornell. First names, geographical terms, bibliography, many other features. 738pp. 4½ x 6¼. T208 Paperbound **$2.00**

MONEY CONVERTER AND TIPPING GUIDE FOR EUROPEAN TRAVEL, C. Vomacka. Invaluable, handy source of currency regulations, conversion tables, tipping rules, postal rates, much other travel information for every European country plus Israel, Egypt and Turkey. 128pp. 3½ x 5¼. T260 Paperbound **60¢**

MONEY CONVERTER AND TIPPING GUIDE FOR TRAVEL IN THE AMERICAS (including the United States and Canada), **C. Vomacka.** The information you need for informed and confident travel in the Americas: money conversion tables, tipping guide, postal, telephone rates, etc. 128pp. 3½ x 5¼. T261 Paperbound **65¢**

DUTCH-ENGLISH, ENGLISH-DUTCH DICTIONARY, F. G. Renier. The most convenient, practical Dutch-English dictionary on the market. New orthography. More than 60,000 entries: idioms, compounds, technical terms, etc. Gender of nouns indicated. xviii + 571pp. 5½ x 6¼. T224 Clothbound **$2.50**

LEARN DUTCH!, F. G. Renier. The most satisfactory and easily-used grammar of modern Dutch. Used and recommended by the Fulbright Committee in the Netherlands. Over 1200 simple exercises lead to mastery of spoken and written Dutch. Dutch-English, English-Dutch vocabularies. 181pp. 4¼ x 7¼. T441 Clothbound **$1.75**

PHRASE AND SENTENCE DICTIONARY OF SPOKEN RUSSIAN, English-Russian, Russian-English. Based on phrases and complete sentences, rather than isolated words; recognized as one of the best methods of learning the idiomatic speech of a country. Over 11,500 entries, indexed by single words, with more than 32,000 English and Russian sentences and phrases, in immediately usable form. Probably the largest list ever published. Shows accent changes in conjugation and declension; irregular forms listed in both alphabetical place and under main form of word. 15,000 word introduction covering Russian sounds, writing, grammar, syntax. 15-page appendix of geographical names, money, important signs, given names, foods, special Soviet terms, etc. Travellers, businessmen, students, government employees have found this their best source for Russian expressions. Originally published as U.S. Government Technical Manual TM 30-944. iv + 573pp. 5⅝ x 8⅜. T496 Paperbound **$2.75**

PHRASE AND SENTENCE DICTIONARY OF SPOKEN SPANISH, Spanish-English, English-Spanish. Compiled from spoken Spanish, emphasizing idiom and colloquial usage in both Castilian and Latin-American. More than 16,000 entries containing over 25,000 idioms—the largest list of idiomatic constructions ever published. Complete sentences given, indexed under single words —language in immediately usable form, for travellers, businessmen, students, etc. 25-page introduction provides rapid survey of sounds, grammar, syntax, with full consideration of irregular verbs. Especially apt in modern treatment of phrases and structure. 17-page glossary gives translations of geographical names, money values, numbers, national holidays, important street signs, useful expressions of high frequency, plus unique 7-page glossary of Spanish and Spanish-American foods and dishes. Originally published as U.S. Government Technical Manual TM 30-900. iv + 513pp. 5⅝ x 8⅜. T495 Paperbound **$1.75**

DOVER BOOKS

ART HISTORY

STICKS AND STONES, Lewis Mumford. An examination of forces influencing American architecture: the medieval tradition in early New England, the classical influence in Jefferson's time, the Brown Decades, the imperial facade, the machine age, etc. "A truly remarkable book," SAT. REV. OF LITERATURE. 2nd revised edition. 21 illus. xvii + 228pp. 5⅜ x 8.
T202 Paperbound $1.60

THE AUTOBIOGRAPHY OF AN IDEA, Louis Sullivan. The architect whom Frank Lloyd Wright called "the master," records the development of the theories that revolutionized America's skyline. 34 full-page plates of Sullivan's finest work. New introduction by R. M. Line. xiv + 335pp. 5⅜ x 8.
T281 Paperbound $1.85

THE MATERIALS AND TECHNIQUES OF MEDIEVAL PAINTING, D. V. Thompson. An invaluable study of carriers and grounds, binding media, pigments, metals used in painting, al fresco and al secco techniques, burnishing, etc. used by the medieval masters. Preface by Bernard Berenson. 239pp. 5⅜ x 8.
T327 Paperbound $1.85

PRINCIPLES OF ART HISTORY, H. Wölfflin. This remarkably instructive work demonstrates the tremendous change in artistic conception from the 14th to the 18th centuries, by analyzing 164 works by Botticelli, Dürer, Hobbema, Holbein, Hals, Titian, Rembrandt, Vermeer, etc., and pointing out exactly what is meant by "baroque," "classic," "primitive," "picturesque," and other basic terms of art history and criticism. "A remarkable lesson in the art of seeing," SAT. REV. OF LITERATURE. Translated from the 7th German edition. 150 illus. 254pp. 6⅛ x 9¼.
T276 Paperbound $2.00

FOUNDATIONS OF MODERN ART, A. Ozenfant. Stimulating discussion of human creativity from paleolithic cave painting to modern painting, architecture, decorative arts. Fully illustrated with works of Gris, Lipchitz, Leger, Picasso, primitive, modern artifacts, architecture, industrial art, much more. 226 illustrations. 368pp. 6⅛ x 9¼.
T215 Paperbound $1.95

HANDICRAFTS, APPLIED ART, ART SOURCES, ETC.

WILD FOWL DECOYS, J. Barber. The standard work on this fascinating branch of folk art, ranging from Indian mud and grass devices to realistic wooden decoys. Discusses styles, types, periods; gives full information on how to make decoys. 140 illustrations (including 14 new plates) show decoys and provide full sets of plans for handicrafters, artists, hunters, and students of folk art. 281pp. 7⅞ x 10¾. Deluxe edition.
T11 Clothbound $8.50

METALWORK AND ENAMELLING, H. Maryon. Probably the best book ever written on the subject. Tells everything necessary for the home manufacture of jewelry, rings, ear pendants, bowls, etc. Covers materials, tools, soldering, filigree, setting stones, raising patterns, repoussé work, damascening, niello, cloisonné, polishing, assaying, casting, and dozens of other techniques. The best substitute for apprenticeship to a master metalworker. 363 photos and figures. 374pp. 5½ x 8½.
T183 Clothbound $7.50

SHAKER FURNITURE, E. D. and F. Andrews. The most illuminating study of Shaker furniture ever written. Covers chronology, craftsmanship, houses, shops, etc. Includes over 200 photographs of chairs, tables, clocks, beds, benches, etc. "Mr. & Mrs. Andrews know all there is to know about Shaker furniture," Mark Van Doren, NATION. 48 full-page plates. 192pp. Deluxe cloth binding. 7⅞ x 10¾.
T7 Clothbound $6.00

PRIMITIVE ART, Franz Boas. A great American anthropologist covers theory, technical virtuosity, styles, symbolism, patterns, etc. of primitive art. The more than 900 illustrations will interest artists, designers, craftworkers. Over 900 illustrations. 376pp. 5⅜ x 8.
T25 Paperbound $1.95

ON THE LAWS OF JAPANESE PAINTING, H. Bowie. The best possible substitute for lessons from an oriental master. Treats both spirit and technique; exercises for control of the brush; inks, brushes, colors; use of dots, lines to express whole moods, etc. 220 illus. 132pp. 6⅛ x 9¼.
T30 Paperbound $1.95

HANDBOOK OF ORNAMENT, F. S. Meyer. One of the largest collections of copyright-free traditional art: over 3300 line cuts of Greek, Roman, Medieval, Renaissance, Baroque, 18th and 19th century art motifs (tracery, geometric elements, flower and animal motifs, etc.) and decorated objects (chairs, thrones, weapons, vases, jewelry, armor, etc.). Full text. 3300 illustrations. 562pp. 5⅜ x 8.
T302 Paperbound $2.00

THREE CLASSICS OF ITALIAN CALLIGRAPHY. Oscar Ogg, ed. Exact reproductions of three famous Renaissance calligraphic works: Arrighi's OPERINA and IL MODO, Tagliente's LO PRESENTE LIBRO, and Palatino's LIBRO NUOVO. More than 200 complete alphabets, thousands of lettered specimens, in Papal Chancery and other beautiful, ornate handwriting. Introduction. 245 plates. 282pp. 6⅛ x 9¼.
T212 Paperbound $1.95

THE HISTORY AND TECHNIQUES OF LETTERING, A. Nesbitt. A thorough history of lettering from the ancient Egyptians to the present, and a 65-page course in lettering for artists. Every major development in lettering history is illustrated by a complete alphabet. Fully analyzes such masters as Caslon, Koch, Garamont, Jenson, and many more. 89 alphabets, 165 other specimens. 317pp. 5⅜ x 8.
T427 Paperbound $2.00

LETTERING AND ALPHABETS, J. A. Cavanagh. An unabridged reissue of "Lettering," containing the full discussion, analysis, illustration of 89 basic hand lettering tyles based on Caslon, Bodoni, Gothic, many other types. Hundreds of technical hints on construction, strokes, pens, brushes, etc. 89 alphabets, 72 lettered specimens, which may be reproduced permission-free. 121pp. 9¾ x 8. T53 Paperbound **$1.25**

THE HUMAN FIGURE IN MOTION, Eadweard Muybridge. The largest collection in print of Muybridge's famous high-speed action photos. 4789 photographs in more than 500 action-strip-sequences (at shutter speeds up to 1/6000th of a second) illustrate men, women, children—mostly undraped—performing such actions as walking, running, getting up, lying down, carrying objects, throwing, etc. "An unparalleled dictionary of action for all artists," AMERICAN ARTIST. 390 full-page plates, with 4789 photographs. Heavy glossy stock, reinforced binding with headbands. 7⅞ x 10¾. T204 Clothbound **$10.00**

ANIMALS IN MOTION, Eadweard Muybridge. The largest collection of animal action photos in print. 34 different animals (horses, mules, oxen, goats, camels, pigs, cats, lions, gnus, deer, monkeys, eagles—and 22 others) in 132 characteristic actions. All 3919 photographs are taken in series at speeds up to 1/1600th of a second, offering artists, biologists, cartoonists a remarkable opportunity to see exactly how an ostrich's head bobs when running, how a lion puts his foot down, how an elephant's knee bends, how a bird flaps his wings, thousands of other hard-to-catch details. "A really marvelous series of plates," NATURE. 380 full-pages of plates. Heavy glossy stock, reinforced binding with headbands. 7⅞ x 10¾. T203 Clothbound **$10.00**

THE BOOK OF SIGNS, R. Koch. 493 symbols—crosses, monograms, astrological, biological symbols, runes, etc.—from ancient manuscripts, cathedrals, coins, catacombs, pottery. May be reproduced permission-free. 493 illustrations by Fritz Kredel. 104pp. 6⅛ x 9¼. T162 Paperbound **$1.00**

A HANDBOOK OF EARLY ADVERTISING ART, C. P. Hornung. The largest collection of copyright-free early advertising art ever compiled. Vol. I: 2,000 illustrations of animals, old automobiles, buildings, allegorical figures, fire engines, Indians, ships, trains, more than 33 other categories! Vol II: Over 4,000 typographical specimens; 600 Roman, Gothic, Barnum, Old English faces; 630 ornamental type faces; hundreds of scrolls, initials, flourishes, etc. "A remarkable collection," PRINTERS' INK.

Vol. I: Pictorial Volume. Over 2000 illustrations. 256pp. 9 x 12. T122 Clothbound **$10.00**
Vol. II: Typographical Volume. Over 4000 speciments. 319pp. 9 x 12. T123 Clothbound **$10.00**
Two volume set, Clothbound, only **$18.50**

DESIGN FOR ARTISTS AND CRAFTSMEN, L. Wolchonok. The most thorough course on the creation of art motifs and designs. Shows you step-by-step, with hundreds of examples and 113 detailed exercises, how to create original designs from geometric patterns, plants, birds, animals, humans, and man-made objects. "A great contribution to the field of design and crafts," N. Y. SOCIETY OF CRAFTSMEN. More than 1300 entirely new illustrations. xv + 207pp. 7⅞ x 10¾. T274 Clothbound **$4.95**

HANDBOOK OF DESIGNS AND DEVICES, C. P. Hornung. A remarkable working collection of 1836 basic designs and variations, all copyright-free. Variations of circle, line, cross, diamond, swastika, star, scroll, shield, many more. Notes on symbolism. "A necessity to every designer who would be original without having to labor heavily," ARTIST and ADVERTISER. 204 plates. 240pp. 5⅜ x 8.
T125 Paperbound **$1.90**

THE UNIVERSAL PENMAN, George Bickham. Exact reproduction of beautiful 18th century book of handwriting. 22 complete alphabets in finest English roundhand, other scripts, over 2000 elaborate flourishes, 122 calligraphic illustrations, etc. Material is copyright-free. "An essential part of any art library, and a book of permanent value," AMERICAN ARTIST. 212 plates. 224pp. 9 x 13¾. T20 Clothbound **$10.00**

AN ATLAS OF ANATOMY FOR ARTISTS, F. Schider. This standard work contains 189 full-page plates, more than 647 illustrations of all aspects of the human skeleton, musculature, cutaway portions of the body, each part of the anatomy, hand forms, eyelids, breasts, location of muscles under the flesh, etc. 59 plates illustrate how Michelangelo, da Vinci, Goya, 15 others, drew human anatomy. New 3rd edition enlarged by 52 new illustrations by Cloquet, Barcsay. "The standard reference tool," AMERICAN LIBRARY ASSOCIATION. "Excellent," AMERICAN ARTIST. 189 plates, 647 illustrations. xxvi + 192pp. 7⅞ x 10⅝. T241 Clothbound **$6.00**

AN ATLAS OF ANIMAL ANATOMY FOR ARTISTS, W. Ellenberger, H. Baum, H. Dittrich. The largest, richest animal anatomy for artists in English. Form, musculature, tendons, bone structure, expression, detailed cross sections of head, other features, of the horse, lion, dog, cat, deer, seal, kangaroo, cow, bull, goat, monkey, hare, many other animals. "Highly recommended," DESIGN. Second, revised, enlarged edition with new plates from Cuvier, Stubbs, etc. 288 illustrations. 153pp. 11⅜ x 9. T82 Clothbound **$6.00**

ANIMAL DRAWING: ANATOMY AND ACTION FOR ARTISTS, C. R. Knight. 158 studies, with full accompanying text, of such animals as the gorilla, bear, bison, dromedary, camel, vulture, pelican, iguana, shark, etc., by one of the greatest modern masters of animal drawing. Innumerable tips on how to get life expression into your work. "An excellent reference work,' SAN FRANCISCO CHRONICLE. 158 illustrations. 156pp. 10½ x 8½.
T426 Paperbound **$2.00**

DOVER BOOKS

THE CRAFTSMAN'S HANDBOOK, Cennino Cennini. The finest English translation of IL LIBRO DELL' ARTE, the 15th century introduction to art technique that is both a mirror of Quatrocento life and a source of many useful but ·nearly forgotten facets of the painter's art. 4 illustrations. xxvii + 142pp. D. V. Thompson, translator. 6⅛ x 9¼.　　T54 Paperbound $1.50

THE BROWN DECADES, Lewis Mumford. A picture of the "buried renaissance" of the post-Civil War period, and the founding of modern architecture (Sullivan, Richardson, Root, Roebling), landscape development (Marsh, Olmstead, Eliot), and the graphic arts (Homer, Eakins, Ryder). 2nd revised, enlarged edition. Bibliography. 12 illustrations. xiv + 266 pp. 5⅜ x 8.　　T200 Paperbound $1.65

STIEGEL GLASS, F. W. Hunter. The story of the most highly esteemed early American glassware, fully illustrated. How a German adventurer, "Baron" Stiegel, founded a glass empire; detailed accounts of individual glasswork. "This pioneer work is reprinted in an edition even more beautiful than the original," ANTIQUES DEALER. New introduction by Helen McKearin. 171 illustrations, 12 in full color. xxii + 338pp. 7⅞ x 10¾.
　　T128 Clothbound $10.00

THE HUMAN FIGURE, J. H. Vanderpoel. Not just a picture book, but a complete course by a famous figure artist. Extensive text, illustrated by 430 pencil and charcoal drawings of both male and female anatomy. 2nd enlarged edition. Foreword. 430 illus. 143pp. 6⅛ x 9¼.
　　T432 Paperbound $1.45

PINE FURNITURE OF EARLY NEW ENGLAND, R. H. Kettell. Over 400 illustrations, over 50 working drawings of early New England chairs, benches, beds cupboards, mirrors, shelves, tables, other furniture esteemed for simple beauty and character. "Rich store of illustrations . . . emphasizes the individuality and varied design," ANTIQUES. 413 illustrations, 55 working drawings. 475pp. 8 x 10¾.　　T145 Clothbound $10.00

BASIC BOOKBINDING, A. W. Lewis. Enables both beginners and experts to rebind old books or bind paperbacks in hard covers. Treats materials, tools; gives step-by-step instruction in how to collate a book, sew it, back it, make boards, etc. 261 illus. Appendices. 155pp. 5⅜ x 8.　　T169 Paperbound $1.35

DESIGN MOTIFS OF ANCIENT MEXICO, J. Enciso. Nearly 90% of these 766 superb designs from Aztec, Olmec, Totonac, Maya, and Toltec origins are unobtainable elsewhere! Contains plumed serpents, wind gods, animals, demons, dancers, monsters, etc. Excellent applied design source. Originally $17.50. 766 illustrations, thousands of motifs. 192pp. 6⅛ x 9¼.
　　T84 Paperbound $1.85

AFRICAN SCULPTURE, Ladislas Segy. 163 full-page plates illustrating masks, fertility figures, ceremonial objects, etc., of 50 West and Central African tribes—95% never before illustrated. 34-page introduction to African sculpture. "Mr. Segy is one of its top authorities," NEW YORKER. 164 full-page photographic plates. Introduction. Bibliography. 244pp. 6⅛ x 9¼.
　　T396 Paperbound $2.00

THE PROCESSES OF GRAPHIC REPRODUCTION IN PRINTING, H. Curwen. A thorough and practical survey of wood, linoleum, and rubber engraving; copper engraving; drypoint, mezzotint, etching, aquatint, steel engraving, die sinking, stencilling, lithography (extensively); photographic reproduction utilizing line, continuous tone, photoengravure, collotype; every other process in general use. Note on color reproduction. Section on bookbinding. Over 200 illustrations, 25 in color. 143pp. 5½ x 8½.　　T512 Clothbound $4.00

CALLIGRAPHY, J. G. Schwandner. First reprinting in 200 years of this legendary book of beautiful handwriting. Over 300 ornamental initials, 12 complete calligraphic alphabets, over 150 ornate frames and panels, 75 calligraphic pictures of cherubs, stags, lions, etc., thousands of flourishes, scrolls, etc., by the greatest 18th century masters. All material can be copied or adapted without permission. Historical introduction. 158 full-page plates. 368pp. 9 x 13.　　T475 Clothbound $10.00

* * *

A DIDEROT PICTORIAL ENCYCLOPEDIA OF TRADES AND INDUSTRY, Manufacturing and the Technical Arts in Plates Selected from "L'Encyclopédie ou Dictionnaire Raisonné des Sciences, des Arts, et des Métiers," of Denis Diderot, edited with text by C. Gillispie. Over 2000 illustrations on 485 full-page plates. Magnificent 18th century engravings of men, women, and children working at such trades as milling flour, cheesemaking, charcoal burning, mining, silverplating, shoeing horses, making fine glass, printing, hundreds more, showing details of machinery, different steps in sequence, etc. A remarkable art work, but also the largest collection of working figures in print, copyright-free, for art directors, designers, etc. Two vols. 920pp. 9 x 12. Heavy library cloth.　　T421 Two volume set $18.50

* * *

SILK SCREEN TECHNIQUES, J. Biegeleisen, M. Cohn. A practical step-by-step home course in one of the most versatile, least expensive graphic arts processes. How to build an inexpensive silk screen, prepare stencils, print, achieve special textures, use color, etc. Every step explained, diagrammed. 149 illustrations, 8 in color. 201pp. 6⅛ x 9¼.
　　T433 Paperbound $1.45

MATHEMATICS, MAGIC AND MYSTERY, Martin Gardner. Astonishing feats of mind reading, mystifying "magic" tricks, are often based on mathematical principles anyone can learn: This book shows you how to perform scores of tricks with cards, dice, coins, knots, numbers, etc., by using simple principles from set theory, theory of numbers, topology, other areas of mathematics, fascinating in themselves. No special knowledge required. 135 illus. 186pp. 5⅜ x 8.
T335 Paperbound **$1.00**

MATHEMATICAL PUZZLES FOR BEGINNERS AND ENTHUSIASTS, G. Mott-Smoth. Test your problem-solving techniques and powers of inference on 188 challenging, amusing puzzles based on algebra, dissection of plane figures, permutations, probabilities, etc. Appendix of primes, square roots, etc. 135 illus. 2nd revised edition. 248pp. 5⅜ x 8.
T198 Paperbound **$1.00**

LEARN CHESS FROM THE MASTERS, F. Reinfeld. Play 10 games against Marshall, Bronstein, Najdorf, other masters, and grade yourself on each move. Detailed annotations reveal principles of play, strategy, etc. as you proceed. An excellent way to get a real insight into the game. Formerly titled, "Chess by Yourself." 91 diagrams. vii + 144pp. 5⅜ x 8.
T362 Paperbound **$1.00**

REINFELD ON THE END GAME IN CHESS, F. Reinfeld. 62 end games of Alekhine, Tarrasch, Morphy, other masters, are carefully analyzed with emphasis on transition from middle game to end play. Tempo moves, queen endings, weak squares, other basic principles clearly illustrated. Excellent for understanding why some moves are weak or incorrect, how to avoid errors. Formerly titled, "Practical End-game Play." 62 diagrams. vi + 177pp. 5⅜ x 8.
T417 Paperbound **$1.25**

101 PUZZLES IN THOUGHT AND LOGIC, C. R. Wylie, Jr. Brand new puzzles you need no special knowledge to solve! Each one is a gem of ingenuity that will really challenge your problem-solving technique. Introduction with simplified explanation of scientic puzzle solving. 128pp. 5⅜ x 8.
T167 Paperbound **$1.00**

THE COMPLETE NONSENSE OF EDWARD LEAR. The only complete edition of this master of gentle madness at a popular price. The Dong with the Luminous Nose, The Jumblies, The Owl and the Pussycat, hundreds of other bits of wonderful nonsense. 214 limericks, 3 sets of Nonsense Botany, 5 Nonsense Alphabets, 546 fantastic drawings, much more. 320pp. 5⅜ x 8.
T167 Paperbound **$1.00**

28 SCIENCE FICTION STORIES OF H. G. WELLS. Two complete novels, "Men Like Gods" and "Star Begotten," plus 26 short stories by the master science-fiction writer of all time. Stories of space, time, future adventure that are among the all-time classics of science fiction. 928pp. 5⅜ x 8.
T265 Clothbound **$3.95**

SEVEN SCIENCE FICTION NOVELS, H. G. Wells. Unabridged texts of "The Time Machine," "The Island of Dr. Moreau," "First Men in the Moon," "The Invisible Man," "The War of the Worlds," "The Food of the Gods," "In the Days of the Comet." "One will have to go far to match this for entertainment, excitement, and sheer pleasure," N. Y. TIMES. 1015pp. 5⅜ x 8.
T264 Clothbound **$3.95**

MATHEMAGIC, MAGIC PUZZLES, AND GAMES WITH NUMBERS, R. V. Heath. More than 60 new puzzles and stunts based on number properties: multiplying large numbers mentally, finding the date of any day in the year, etc. Edited by J. S. Meyer. 76 illus. 129pp. 5⅜ x 8.
T110 Paperbound **$1.00**

FIVE ADVENTURE NOVELS OF H. RIDER HAGGARD. The master story-teller's five best tales of mystery and adventure set against authentic African backgrounds: "She," "King Solomon's Mines," "Allan Quatermain," "Allan's Wife," "Maiwa's Revenge." 821pp. 5⅜ x 8.
T108 Clothbound **$3.95**

WIN AT CHECKERS, M. Hopper. (Formerly "Checkers.") The former World's Unrestricted Checker Champion gives you valuable lessons in openings, traps, end games, ways to draw when you are behind, etc. More than 100 questions and answers anticipate your problems. Appendix. 75 problems diagrammed, solved. 79 figures. xi + 107pp. 5⅜ x 8.
T363 Paperbound **$1.00**

CRYPTOGRAPHY, L. D. Smith. Excellent introductory work on ciphers and their solution, history of secret writing, techniques, etc. Appendices on Japanese methods, the Baconian cipher, frequency tables. Bibliography. Over 150 problems, solutions. 160pp. 5⅜ x 8.
T247 Paperbound **$1.00**

CRYPTANALYSIS, H. F. Gaines. (Formerly, "Elementary Cryptanalysis.") The best book available on cryptograms and how to solve them. Contains all major techniques: substitution, transposition, mixed alphabets, multafid, Kasiski and Vignere methods, etc. Word frequency appendix. 167 problems, solutions. 173 figures. 236pp. 5⅜ x 8.
T97 Paperbound **$1.95**

FLATLAND, E. A. Abbot. The science-fiction classic of life in a 2-dimensional world that is considered a first-rate introduction to relativity and hyperspace, as well as a scathing satire on society, politics and religion. 7th edition. 16 illus. 128pp. 5⅜ x 8.
T1 Paperbound **$1.00**

DOVER BOOKS

HOW TO FORCE CHECKMATE, F. Reinfeld. (Formerly "Challenge to Chessplayers.") No board needed to sharpen your checkmate skill on 300 checkmate situations. Learn to plan up to 3 moves ahead and play a superior end game. 300 situations diagrammed; notes and full solutions. 111pp. 5⅜ x 8.   T439 Paperbound **$1.25**

MORPHY'S GAMES OF CHESS, P. W. Sergeant, ed. Play forcefully by following the techniques used by one of the greatest chess champions. 300 of Morphy's games carefully annotated to reveal principles. Bibliography. New introduction by F. Reinfeld. 235 diagrams. x + 352pp. 5⅜ x 8.   T386 Paperbound **$1.75**

MATHEMATICAL RECREATIONS, M. Kraitchik. Hundreds of unusual mathematical puzzlers and odd bypaths of math, elementary and advanced. Greek, Medieval, Arabic, Hindu problems; figurate numbers, Fermat numbers, primes; magic, Euler, Latin squares; fairy chess, latruncles, reversi, jinx, ruma, tetrachrome other positional and permutational games. Rigorous solutions. Revised second edition. 181 illus. 330pp. 5⅜ x 8.   T163 Paperbound **$1.75**

MATHEMATICAL EXCURSIONS, H. A. Merrill. Revealing stimulating insights into elementary math, not usually taught in school. 90 problems demonstrate Russian peasant multiplication, memory systems for pi, magic squares, dyadic systems, division by inspection, many more. Solutions to difficult problems. 50 illus. 5⅜ x 8.   T350 Paperbound **$1.00**

MAGIC TRICKS & CARD TRICKS, W. Jonson. Best introduction to tricks with coins, bills, eggs, ribbons, slates, cards, easily performed without elaborate equipment. Professional routines, tips on presentation, misdirection, etc. Two books bound as one: 52 tricks with cards, 37 tricks with common objects. 106 figures. 224pp. 5⅜ x 8.   T909 Paperbound **$1.00**

MATHEMATICAL PUZZLES OF SAM LOYD, selected and edited by **M. Gardner.** 177 most ingenious mathematical puzzles of America's greatest puzzle originator, based on arithmetic, algebra, game theory, dissection, route tracing, operations research, probability, etc. 120 drawings, diagrams. Solutions. 187pp. 5⅜ x 8.   T498 Paperbound **$1.00**

THE ART OF CHESS, J. Mason. The most famous general study of chess ever written. More than 90 openings, middle game, end game, how to attack, sacrifice, defend, exchange, form general strategy. Supplement on "How Do You Play Chess?" by F. Reinfeld. 448 diagrams. 356pp. 5⅜ x 8.   T463 Paperbound **$1.85**

HYPERMODERN CHESS as Developed in the Games of its Greatest Exponent, ARON NIMZOVICH, F. Reinfeld, ed. Learn how the game's greatest innovator defeated Alekhine, Lasker, and many others; and use these methods in your own game. 180 diagrams. 228pp. 5⅜ x 8.
                                                         T448 Paperbound **$1.35**

A TREASURY OF CHESS LORE, F. Reinfeld, ed. Hundreds of fascinating stories by and about the masters, accounts of tournaments and famous games, aphorisms, word portraits, little known incidents, photographs, etc., that will delight the chess enthusiast, captivate the beginner. 49 photographs (14 full-page plates), 12 diagrams. 315pp. 5⅜ x 8.
                                                         T458 Paperbound **$1.75**

A NONSENSE ANTHOLOGY, collected by **Carolyn Wells.** 245 of the best nonsense verses ever written: nonsense puns, absurd arguments, mock epics, nonsense ballads, "sick" verses, dog-Latin verses, French nonsense verses, limericks. Lear, Carroll, Belloc, Burgess, nearly 100 other writers. Introduction by Carolyn Wells. 3 indices: Title, Author, First Lines. xxxiii + 279pp. 5⅜ x 8.   T499 Paperbound **$1.25**

SYMBOLIC LOGIC and THE GAME OF LOGIC, Lewis Carroll. Two delightful puzzle books by the author of "Alice," bound as one. Both works concern the symbolic representation of traditional logic and together contain more than 500 ingenious, amusing and instructive syllogistic puzzlers. Total of 326pp. 5⅜ x 8.   T492 Paperbound **$1.50**

PILLOW PROBLEMS and A TANGLED TALE, Lewis Carroll. Two of Carroll's rare puzzle works bound as one. "Pillow Problems" contain 72 original math puzzles. The puzzles in "A Tangled Tale" are given in delightful story form. Total of 291pp. 5⅜ x 8.   T493 Paperbound **$1.50**

PECK'S BAD BOY AND HIS PA, G. W. Peck. Both volumes of one of the most widely read of all American humor books. A classic of American folk humor, also invaluable as a portrait of an age. 100 original illustrations. Introduction by E. Bleiler. 347pp. 5⅜ x 8.
                                                         T497 Paperbound **$1.35**
